**CREATE ONCE,
DISTRIBUTE FOREVER**

CREATE ONCE, DISTRIBUTE FOREVER

HOW GREAT CREATORS SPREAD THEIR IDEAS AND HOW YOU CAN TOO

ROSS SIMMONDS

LIONCREST
PUBLISHING

CREATE ONCE, DISTRIBUTE FOREVER
How Great Creators Spread Their Ideas and How You Can Too
First Edition

ISBN   978-1-5445-4129-7   *Hardcover*
      978-1-5445-4127-3   *Paperback*
      978-1-5445-4128-0   *Ebook*

To Kris, Aaliyah, Isabelle and Reggie

The battle comes down to whether
the startup gets distribution before
the incumbent gets innovation.

—ALEX RAMPELL

General Partner at Andreessen Horowitz

CONTENTS

PART III. CHANNEL-BY-CHANNEL GUIDE

PART IV. THE PLAYBOOK

INTRODUCTION

"Content is king." Bill Gates said these three words once, and for years to follow, gurus on the internet and at conferences have preached these three words like they were the answer to every marketing problem. The message is always some version of the same thing: "Create more content and revenue will follow." Creating more content has become the purported fix for almost all growth problems. Want to increase traffic? Generate more users? Get more podcast listeners? Improve your followers on social media? Increase your overall market share? Just create more content and, ipso facto, the results naturally follow.

This narrative about content is wrong and not rooted in whole truths. And underneath it all, you probably know it just as well as I do.

It doesn't take an extensive internet search to find brilliant creators, artists, entrepreneurs, or marketers who have developed excellent work with industry-changing ideas, culture-shaping messages, or stories worth sharing. Yet, no one is looking at, reading, or listening to their work. They put in the time and effort, but engagement with their posts, videos, essays, and announcements is disproportionately low compared to the quality. The content is published but met with nothing but crickets.

For these folks—and you may be one of them—it's not clear how to distribute effectively or how to attract more people to their work, app, product, job board, or digital course. What these folks don't realize is that *how and where* their work is shared is now more important than just creating it.

A paradigm is shifting. Creating is no longer enough. You need to embrace distribution. The good news is this: Distribution is almost impossible to take from someone once it's been cracked. Once you have sustainable distribution, you have an unfair advantage, and that's exactly why it should be pursued aggressively and intentionally. It's why you picked up this book. Deep down, you know that distribution is one of the greatest forces in business yet arguably one of the most misunderstood. Today, I can reach millions of people and earn millions of dollars without dropping a penny on paid media because of the distribution channels I've built.

This book is my attempt to arm you with that same power of distribution. I'm going to be focused primarily on the distribution of content, but in most cases you can swap that idea for almost anything you create online. Products. Businesses. Art. Podcasts. Videos. Stories. You name it. This is the book about distribution I wish I had before I wasted thousands of hours creating things for the sake of creating them. This is the book that will show you the power of creating something once and distributing it forever.

THE POWER OF AN AUDIENCE

Why do so many great creations fall flat instead of reaching their full potential? A lot of creators forget all about the importance of finding and reaching their audience. When speaking in an empty theater, there are no ears to listen. Great content cannot reach its full potential unless spread in full theaters or, better yet, on the right channels where an ideal audience is waiting. Yes, it's great that you developed something that is valuable, insightful, and even helpful. But as creators, isn't that what you're supposed to do?

I'm so tired of seeing creators brag about how they set a high bar for what they create. You see it online every day in both the office and online. Creators talk about their great content but that it's not their fault that people aren't seeing their greatness. Give me a break. You don't get applause for creating valuable content. But for some reason, teams and organizations around the globe applaud their teams just because they press publish for creating something good.

It's a dilemma that reminds me of an old Chris Rock joke. He jokes that a lot of dads brag that they're in their kids' lives and sometimes even expect applause for raising their kids. But that's nonsense, he argues, because raising your kids is what you're supposed to do. You don't get applause for doing what you're supposed to do! Similarly, creators shouldn't expect applause just for creating good things. That's what you're supposed to do. What elevates the best creators from the rest is the distribution.

I look at creators, builders, and writers all over the globe and often feel bad. An unfortunate truth is that today some of the most fascinating and important pieces of work will never impact or improve people around the world because the creators will never get their heads out of the sand and provide their work with the distribution it deserves.

Perhaps you are an early-stage startup founder with an excellent product. Perhaps you are a content marketer with industry-changing content. But, you don't know how to effectively distribute your work—it's outside the realm of your expertise. Or, perhaps, you think you need a huge marketing budget (you don't). Whatever the case, your work is not selling well. Your content has little engagement. And the podcast you have been investing in for months only has a handful of listeners (most of them being your team, investors, and friends).

This can be frustrating. You are putting time, effort, and energy into something but have little to show for it. What's more, sitting on content that the world would benefit from means your good ideas are going unused twice; neither you nor the consumer reap the rewards.

And for some, it can be uncomfortable promoting one-self. I get it. But your great ideas won't share themselves. I'm willing to bet that right now, you probably have great content. It's valuable to somebody out there, but because your content hasn't been promoted and distributed effectively, it's collecting dust. Worse yet, it may never realize its full potential. In fact, it might reach its full potential someday but at a time when you're not even around to see that happen. Morbid I know. But the truth hurts.

Hundreds of artists never see the praise and admiration that fans give their work simply because they didn't have the distribution channels necessary to succeed before their death. I'm hoping that this book is going to arm you with the insurance to not fall into the same trap.

FROM POTENTIAL GROWTH TO REALIZED GROWTH

It was 2014, and I was feeling the pressure. I had just signed the paperwork for my first mortgage, something my $40,000 salary was just barely covering. If I wanted to achieve my own entrepreneurial goals and own my time, I needed to make the leap from company worker to self-employed marketer.

It was a nice dream, but on paper it didn't seem feasible. Growing up and living in Preston, Nova Scotia—a town of less than 3,500 residents—the idea of running a business capable of influencing millions and generating millions felt out of reach, especially considering the fact that I didn't have high-speed internet until I was sixteen. To find any success, it became a priority for me to build relationships with people outside of my neighborhood.

Living on the East Coast of Canada with a small network and hardly any direction, how was I going to break into the professional spaces that would launch my company? Thankfully, a university hobby gave me the answer. I ran a fantasy football blog that became ridiculously popular and built a following online. To my surprise, my posts about who people should start or sit in their fantasy lineups were being shared by hundreds and redistributed by thousands, creating opportunities for me to make ad money.

In time, my earnings helped pay off school. Tuition was covered simply because my content was being read and shared time after time. But the most successful pieces were those that were getting featured by some of the biggest names in Fantasy Sports at the time. And that's when it quickly became crystal clear to me: distribution was the key.

As my hobby gave way to running my own business, my content shifted to marketing. Early on, my content was only shared and liked by my mom—shoutout to all of the supportive moms out there—and a few friends. Then, one evening, I tested some distribution waters by carefully seeding a piece of content into two prominent digital communities (one called Inbound and one called Growth Hackers). Within a matter of minutes, thousands of people had visited my website and my followers on social media exploded.

From a few to a few thousand. To see such growth in a shorter timeframe than it takes to eat lunch was an eye-opening experience. What prompted such a dramatic increase? Did I create new content until something I wrote resonated with the internet? No. In fact, I had used an old piece of content. It was the distribution that acted as the catalyst for a steep uptick in engagement. And that engagement led to opportunities to earn $40,000—what was at one time my annual salary—in two months.

What I discovered was this: Distribution is the most important yet underrated part of business. Over the course of my career, I've also come to learn it's often overlooked by companies, artists, musicians, developers, and creators alike. Distribution through Craigslist helped Airbnb reach millions. Distribution through email signatures helped Hotmail reach millions. And distribution through IBM helped MS-Dos (Microsoft) reach millions. If you are to thrive and let your projects reach their full potential, you need to adopt a distribution-focused strategy.

This book will help you do just that.

CREATE ONCE, DISTRIBUTE FOREVER

The following pages share some of the distribution strategies and techniques that I've used to help brands, founders, entrepreneurs, marketers, and builders distribute their stories, content, and products to the masses. Whether it's leveraging channels like YouTube to reach millions or leveraging search-engine optimization to reach hundreds of millions, the opportunity for distribution is there, and it will change the way you navigate business. You can experience real and scalable growth when proper distribution strategies are realized.

Part 1 will run through an introductory education on distribution—dubbed Distribution 101. This will include a basic understanding of what distribution is and why you should embrace it as a strategy. you'll also discover the roadblocks that prevent people from utilizing distribution, including steps for how to avoid and overcome them. As you learn about fundamental distribution channels, those channels will act as the gateway into the nuanced plans of action explored in future chapters.

In Part 2 we'll look at the importance of remixing and republishing content. Using real-world examples, we'll discuss how successful companies tend to remix their best content in fresh and exciting ways. Content that resonates never goes out of style. Remix and republish it. Give it renewed life to resonate with your audience once again.

Then, in Part 3, you are presented with a choose-your-own-adventure, channel-by-channel guide that covers the gamut of content distribution channels. Thankfully, you come to this experience as an expert in your content or product already. Which chapters will be most relevant and useful for you will depend on which channels are most appropriate for your marketing strategy.

In total, we'll cover email, social media, partnership, community, and search distribution. You can open these chapters time and time again, highlighter at the ready, as you develop your distribution plans. It will be your go-to place to reaffirm or adjust how you distribute content.

And finally, Part 4 offers a Content Distribution Playbook. Not every book provides a clear direction forward. However, here you will find a to-do checklist and an example distribution schedule to get you started. Both will function as part of your playbook, helping you hold fast to a new and successful distribution strategy. Framing these templates is a step-by-step guide to approaching your distribution strategy with utmost efficiency.

In the end, you will have confidence in marketing yourself, your work, and your company. I dare say, you'll even enjoy it because you'll have a data-backed marketing strategy that makes sense *and* works.

Further, you will know exactly where to distribute and how to create maximum reach of your target audience. You will know how your existing content resonates most with your audience and how to use that content in multiple modalities in a way that feels authentic, fresh, and new each time. And last but not least, you will know the steps necessary to increase your engagement on all platforms, such as more social media follows, podcast subscribers, app downloads, and the like.

With this book, you can finally get off the hamster wheel of creating for the sake of creating. You will be able to build a distribution engine that arms you with a profit-scalable and less stressful means to ensure that your work reaches the right people at the right time.

MY GOAL FOR THIS BOOK

Since 2014, my company, Foundation Marketing, has worked with organizations with multi-billion dollar market caps, including some of the fastest-growing startups of all time. As a leader in SaaS (software as a service) marketing, our content on growth, SEO (search engine optimization), content creation, social media, and distribution have reached millions of people all over the world. Our own distribution work and content expertise have helped us capture the attention of the most ambitious brands in the world, including work with software companies that you very likely use on a day-to-day basis to run your operations.

This marketing influence didn't happen overnight, and the insights and lessons in this book derive from having lived these strategies. What you will learn in the pages that follow is rooted in experience, experimentation, and application. I've helped many companies spread their stories, and I want to help you spread your story, too.

My goal for you is to create distribution engines that you can use to accelerate your content's or product's reach, whatever success means for your situation. You, too, can follow the growth footsteps of start-ups-turned-industry-leaders I've helped like Unbounce, a landing page builder and platform. Unbounce's success was fueled, in part, by an excellent distribution strategy. Through Foundation Marketing, we ran a distribution process across their content using the strategies we'll cover in the coming pages. Shortly thereafter, their engagement and traffic increased tenfold—and this growth occurred on the back of content they had previously created.

You may already have all the content you need. You could be sitting on twenty excellent blog posts or pieces of content that didn't get distributed, amplified, or promoted properly or to the right audience. Don't let your assets go to waste. By the end of this book, you'll know what to do with them by creating and implementing a strong distribution strategy.

Now, does this mean you should stop creating content? No. Creating new content is clearly important when it comes to marketing and growth. Continuing to make more and more content, however, will not fix your distribution problem. In fact, it simply means you're spending more time, effort, or money (or a combination of the three) to develop new assets. Instead, reuse, rewrite, update, and amplify what you already have.

The world is already very noisy. More content is not the best way to get noticed. In fact, competitors will see what you've produced and copy it. Or, as I've said in the past, it's easy to copy an idea, but it's hard to copy a distribution strategy. So how do you cut through the noise? That takes work. You have to embrace distribution and marry it to good content.

Speaking of work, if you believe you'll be able to snap your fingers and immediately scale your traffic, followers, or users, this book is not for you. This is not a short-term fix. Distribution takes effort. Setting up a clearly planned and thoughtful distribution strategy is how you uncover opportunities worth chasing, extend your reach, and produce growth.

All of this needs to start with an understanding of what distribution is, which is where we will begin. When you have distribution, you give yourself the opportunity to put your work in front of your ideal audience and ultimately unlock a consistent and sustainable competitive advantage.

Your work needs to stop collecting dust and start collecting results, and I'm thrilled to guide you through the process of creating and unlocking great distribution.

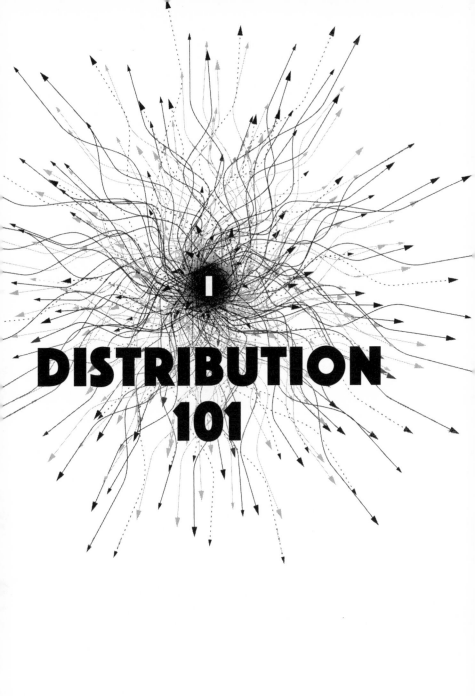

I
DISTRIBUTION 101

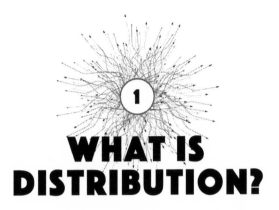

WHAT IS DISTRIBUTION?

HAT'S VIRAL SPREADS, CATCHES ON, AND becomes instantly recognizable.

We saw it with the COVID-19 pandemic. We see it each fall with the flu and the common cold. Every few years, we become aware of a prolific virus spreading, and we have to stay vaccinated or vigilant. Ebola. SARS. Zika. Smallpox. These are but some examples of viruses that have entered our lives, and they make for a great analogy of what great distribution looks like when it's happening and operating in full swing.

The influence of pandemics is real and vast. Never isolated, a virus spreads and spreads, from human to human, and it moves through us until all of humanity is either infected or impacted. Depending on the severity, viral pandemics can change the world. Just think back to your experience in the three or so years of COVID-19. We wore masks, sheltered in place, cleaned our groceries with bleach, and washed our hands while humming "Happy Birthday." Wild times.

What makes a pandemic such a global event? In one word: distribution. It's not so much the virus itself that matters, it's the virus' ability to spread quickly that determines the scope and impact of the given pandemic.

In the business world, distribution very much operates like a viral pandemic. Of course, that is why the term "viral" is associated with business and social media trends. For good or for bad, we see it when TikTok videos explode in popularity (or Instagram Reels if you are older than a certain age). Like a flashbang, the popularity of content can strike through the heart of the internet. If one person with 100,000 followers shares your content, it could be considered a digital equivalent of a super-spreader event.

Well-distributed content can spread around the world in a matter of minutes or even less. The internet means global connectivity. Mere seconds is all it takes. A click here, a swipe there, and content with a significant viral impact can travel the globe instantaneously to shape the minds of millions and billions of people.

The reality is this: one piece of content, when distributed properly, can leave a massive impression on the planet not dissimilar to the game-changing impacts of pandemics. A great piece of content benefiting from great distribution can fundamentally change your life as an individual and the world as a whole. I know this because I have had single pieces of content utilize monthly promotion and distribution strategies to generate well over a million dollars in revenue for my company and change my life.

A well-distributed piece can drastically alter how your company operates. Maybe it increases your traffic, your downloads, or any desired metric that generates new leads and business. With the right distribution engine, the growth, influence, and spread of your content cannot be stopped.

Your content can spread like a virus and morph into new strains. People will translate it into international languages. Others will make graphics to visually aid the material. You published it on Reddit, but your friend saw it on Slack. Another friend texts you a headline from Facebook. It will be transformed into an Instagram post or a TikTok video, and it will cross mediums the likes of which you will have never imagined.

Your content, work, brand, and story can change the world, and that is the power of distribution. When you have the right vehicle—the right distribution—your great content will spread like a virus. It's not so much the content itself or a virus itself that matters most, it's the distributive power of the vehicle that spreads the content. And throughout this book, we will cover the strategies required for you to spread your story all over the world.

DISTRIBUTION IS FOUNDATIONAL

Prior to our earliest communication technologies of smoke signals and carrier pigeons, stories were spread primarily through word of mouth. Even the world's earliest forms of literature were first spread orally. It is believed Homer's *The Iliad* and *The Odyssey*—both considered the first written texts in Western literature—were written an estimated 500 years after the former's subject matter, the Trojan War. That means centuries of passing along both poems through word of mouth. Oral tradition meant passing stories from generation to generation. The texts that survived had a long gestation period, but they nonetheless found distribution channels and continue to circulate to this day.

Much later, humans started utilizing letters and mail carriers. Then they invented the telegraph to communicate over vast distances even faster. Then came the radio and even television. Companies could reach large audiences by buying Super Bowl ads once a year, but that's no longer needed. Now, millions and billions of people are within reach with the click of a button. You can put up a great post on LinkedIn, X (formerly known as Twitter), Facebook, TikTok, Reddit, and many other platforms to reach massive swaths of people.

When tracing a history of communication and consumption, we find two things. First, the capabilities of distribution only increase over time. More and more people are within reach as communication and distribution technology continues to develop. Second, we learn that for something to survive or thrive, it must maintain some semblance of distribution.

Let's return to the concept of virality. Founder and entrepreneur Kevin Kwok once tweeted, "We [have learned] in vaccines what most startups inevitably realize too late. Product is great, but most of the time, you live or die by distribution."[1] In this sense, what Kwon suggests is that for a virus to be stopped, the distributors (a.k.a. humans) need to be taken into consideration.

---

1   Kevin Kwok, Twitter post, January 20, 2021, 12:16 a.m., https:// twitter.com/kevinakwok/status/1351805737727533056/.

Thankfully, distribution of content has never been easier, but it's also never been more valuable. Regular human beings with meager means have the ability to distribute their content at levels that are comparable to media giants with billion-dollar distribution budgets.

There is no better example of distribution's necessity than the newspaper industry. For over a century, and prior to the spread of the internet, newspapers had a lock on distribution by having access to the doorsteps of millions of people all over the world. Their content-distribution strategy consisted of delivering their copy to their readers' door every single day (or once a week, depending on the publication). There were no other channels to consume long-form news and information. Television certainly had news programs, but they had to short-cut the details to keep the half-hour time slot.

As the internet started to become more accessible, people were given the opportunity to consume news whenever they wanted. Soon, that distributive power transferred to their mobile devices. Online news distribution was able to one-up print news. It bypassed the front door and went straight into the consumer's pocket.

With a better distribution strategy, online news prevented print news from standing out. Losing their monopoly on distribution, newsprint has slowly gone the way of the buffalo. On the other hand, online news has thrived. The old-world jobs of journalists and reporters still exist, but they wield their phones and Twitter profiles instead of their typewriters. Competing with them are creators, bloggers, and other folks who have found a way to distribute news content online to niche audiences.

In the history of newspapers, we can demonstrate that distribution has the ability to change everything. Nobody thought that newspapers could ever die. But they did, or, at least, they are still on life support.

DEFINING DISTRIBUTION

Certainly, everybody in the industry will have their own definition of the word *distribute*. Here is how it might look if you were to find it in a regular dictionary.

dis·trib·ute
noun
either to divide among many or to spread out, so
    as to cover something or give out or deliver,
    especially to members of a group.

This is a great place to start, but it is not quite tailored for our purposes. This is how I would define the term in the context of content marketing, an entry in the Ross Simmonds Dictionary of Marketing.

dis·trib·ute

noun

to spread your content, product, or stories to a large
target audience by repurposing or remixing your
content into a wide range of different content
channels and mediums.[2]

At its core, distribution can be defined as taking an asset that you've produced and repurposing it for placement in a number of distribution channels to reach the widest audience possible. Why is leading with a definition an important place to start? Tying distribution to widening the audience helps you embrace the importance of distribution to the success or failure of a given product or piece of content.

And why can we tie distribution to success, not content? It's not necessarily the best product that will win the market. Rather, the best distribution wins. A lot of startups and entrepreneurs make the mistake of allocating their budgets to creating the perfect product or content. They are

---

2   Ross Simmonds, Ross Simmonds Dictionary of Content Marketing
     [Unpublished manuscript]. Publication TBD.

trying to create the next blockbuster film, the next industry-changing software, the most-used app, or anything else
that will dominate the attention of consumers. To a certain
degree, all entrepreneurs, even me, become obsessed with
this idea that we can be part of creating the "next big thing."

What is often overlooked in that recipe are indicator
words revealing that the audience is the most important
ingredient, not the product or content itself. The "most-
used" app has a large audience. An "industry-changing"
piece of software gets that moniker after mass adoption. A
"blockbuster" film suggests that the reach of a film is car-
ried to a huge audience. Effective distribution made these
products successful, not the products themselves.

Over the years, there has been example after example
of mediocre products outselling better quality competitors. Just walk into any grocery store and go to the granola
bar aisle. In that aisle, there's a brand-name, low-qual-
ity granola bar that tastes like cardboard and is made
with unhealthy ingredients. And it sells like gangbusters.
Elsewhere, only one or two local supermarkets might carry
the under-the-radar, delicious, organic, oatmeal bar created by a local producer operating out of a farmer's market,
which very few people buy. The difference between them
is distribution. The bad product wins because it is in more
places and in front of more faces.

I'm also reminded of 2009's blockbuster film, *Avatar*. I'm not saying the film wasn't revolutionary. It was enjoyable, but the distribution was a masterclass. In his press tour, James Cameron spoke openly about the film's at-the-time gigantic budget of $237 million. Cameron revealed that the film's distribution company had nearly the same budget as the film itself. With excellent distribution, Avatar was certain to make its money back. Today, the original Avatar sits as the second highest-grossing film of all time, clearing three-and-a-half billion dollars (adjusted for inflation) in box office sales.

So yeah, they made their money back and then some.

DISTRIBUTION IS SERIOUS BUSINESS

What do granola bars and Hollywood films have to do with you? Right now, there are creators, founders, and entrepreneurs creating startups, top-of-the-line content, blogs, e-books, products, and more, yet they are not leaders in their given market. It's because they've yet to crack the distribution puzzle. Subsequently, their amazing ideas and deserved opportunities go unfulfilled.

If you aren't distributing your work, you might never reap the benefits. What's worse, the people who would have benefitted the most from your content or product never even got the opportunity because they were never reached. You can fundamentally change your own life and the lives of others by distributing your work. That is why distribution is important, and that is why I'm so passionate about this topic. I am convinced that some of the greatest ideas in the world already exist, and you might be holding onto one or more of them. But because you don't know how to distribute it professionally, it might die with you someday.

It doesn't matter where you are right now. Every YouTube channel starts with zero subscribers. If you look at the early days of YouTube, one of its emerging creators was a kid named Justin Bieber. At that time, he was not an internationally known musical phenomenon. His early attempts at spreading his content didn't gain much traction. YouTube, in 2007, was not a major distribution channel for musicians. But, he studied the YouTube ecosystem and generated a wider viewership by learning how to distribute stories on the platform. YouTube distribution landed him in the hands of a music distributor who had access to the proper channels, and the rest is history. Because he understands that distribution is something to embrace forever, Justin Bieber has kept his YouTube channel—which has one of the largest audiences—and continues to post content.

But not everybody is looking for musical stardom. Scalable growth and revenue is the goal of many businesses and founders. Distribution offers that for companies. I might be dating myself with this example, but let's recall the power of distribution for Hotmail, the predecessor of Gmail. They had a default signature set up in users' email accounts. Every time the user sent an email, the bottom signature would read "PS: I love you. Get your free email at Hotmail." This distribution hack gave them the ability to unlock and generate millions of new signups.

Within hours of implementing the signature as a default setting, they saw a hockey-stick curve in growth. Hotmail started with 3,000 users. Within six months, they were up to a million. Five weeks after that, they hit two million. In essence, Hotmail generated free advertising and put their name in front of every recipient of an email from a Hotmail account. It went down as perhaps the most brilliant moment of early-internet content distribution. And it demonstrated the viral power that distribution has in business growth.

DISTRIBUTION IS OFTEN OVERLOOKED

The major mistake most individuals or companies make is to over-obsess the thing they want to distribute. The product is placed over the distribution process. Not enough time is spent thinking about how to spread the content or product, nor the importance of getting it in front of the right people.

Returning to the demise of print news, so many journalists romanticized the importance of physical newspapers. The layout of one story next to another. The tackiness of the ink. The importance of different font sizes on the paper. It's easy to romanticize the past when it has allowed you to reap significant rewards. That makes it easy to push back on burgeoning norms. For print news, the writing was on the wall. Well, that writing was actually in code and in a computer. Yet, many journalists and their employers refused to transition to an online format. That led to the shuttering of hundreds of newspapers across the country. When the product or content is put above distribution, the former usually fails.

Not distributing your work means withholding your solution to a user's pain point. As you read these words, it is very likely that somebody out there is struggling with a problem that *you* have a solution to. You might have an e-book, a product, or a blog post that can help a consumer solve a paint point. But because you haven't spent any time learning how to distribute, that person will continue to struggle. Why haven't you distributed it to them yet?

Perhaps the importance of distribution never crossed your mind. Or maybe you are afraid of your content being judged. These are legitimate concerns and experiences, things I hope to help you address as we continue through this book's lessons. The foundational concept holding everything up, though, is that business failure is often the result of not distributing your content or product.

If you want to unlock the full potential of the assets you're creating, you shouldn't allow your content to collect dust. You must have the ability to create great content, but it has to reach the right people. It's more important than ever to make it spread like a virus.

No matter your industry, no matter the space you work in, no matter where you are in the world, there are people out there who want to consume your content or product. And as you will discover in detail, your audience might be meeting in unexpected places. You have to find their channels and meet them there to display your content.

Every week people use the excuse that their audience isn't on such-and-such channel. For example, accountants might be scared to use social media because their potential customers may perceive them as unprofessional. Therefore, they give up on distribution.

What they fail to recognize is that their audience might be on LinkedIn—a serious, professional social media channel—instead of TikTok (in reality some of them probably are on TikTok, too). On LinkedIn, there are millions of people with any given job title using LinkedIn as a channel to learn, stay connected, and discuss things happening in their profession. Today, LinkedIn has well over eight million users who identify as accountants. Sounds like an excellent opportunity.

If you or anyone says "Our audience is too professional" or "Our audience doesn't spend time on these massive channels," I'm here to say you're wrong. Certainly not all eight million accountants will be the ideal customer. But, even if 1 percent of them were your ideal customer, that means 80,000 people will be interested in what you're selling. That's a pretty good uptick in engagement created by distribution. And this story can be repeated to some degree or another using any niche group. An obscure group like waste management software engineers have their own, exploitable distribution channels.

Anyone can continue down the path of suggesting "distribution might not be for us." But you'll lose out. Your audience exists, and they are waiting for you.

2

WHY YOU SHOULD EMBRACE DISTRIBUTION

M Y FIRST LESSON IN DISTRIBUTION CAME IN HIGH
school. I grew up and lived in a community called
Preston, which is on the outskirts of Halifax, Nova
Scotia. Halifax is a relatively small city with an even
smaller Black population. As one of the few Black people
in Nova Scotia, I happened into a not-often-frequented-
by-Black-people store selling hair products. I noticed they
were selling durags. When I was growing up, durags were

just starting to become popular as Hip Hop artists like 50 Cent, Cam'ron, Ludacris and more brought them into the limelight as a fashion statement.

This store had durags of all different colors: red, yellow, pink, blue, you name it. They had every option. That caught my attention, because local grocery stores would only carry black or white, colors that were guaranteed to sell at higher rates.

I recognized almost immediately that this hair-product store didn't have access to the community I had access to. I had the distribution advantage. This is where I should probably mention that this was pre-internet, so it wasn't a world where anyone could order a durag online. So, I asked my parents for an advance on my allowance and bought them out.

The next day, I hung the durags in my locker at school and sold them at $7.50 a piece, twice what I paid for them. I sold them all by midday. The store I bought them from hadn't sold a single durag in months until I started making regular purchases. I continued to sell the durags consistently, and it provided me with the money to buy my favorite high-school lunch: poutine.

That was my first taste of distribution and entrepreneurship. If you find the right audience, your content can command quite a bit of attention and capital. It's a lesson I continue to implement as a marketing professional. For example, in 2018, I wrote a professional blog for my website called "Why Gangster Rap & Coffee Is The Perfect Recipe For Productivity (Research Backed)." I'm obsessed with coffee. I'm also obsessed with hip-hop. So I created that piece after doing a bit of research and analysis.

Using evidence, my article argued that if you listen to high-tempo music, such as gangster rap, and you drink coffee, your productivity can increase. Interesting, right? I agree. So I put this piece out there. I pressed publish on it with anticipation, as I thought it would be received with amazement. What happened? Crickets.

It didn't generate any engagement at all. Nobody pressed the 'like' button. Nobody shared it. Nobody commented on it. Was it over? Was it time to create a new, better piece of content? No, it wasn't. I decided not to let this piece die or collect dust. I had faith that this was strong content that could influence people. All I needed to do was get it into the right hands.

Doing the sharing on my own, I distributed this piece into a number of communities. I posted it to Hacker News, LinkedIn, Medium, Reddit, Twitter, Facebook, and the like. Depending on the platform, I would share it with niche-specific groups, such as coffee enthusiast groups and "Hip-Hop Heads" on Facebook. By the end of that day, my post had 35,000 views.

Within six months, it took off. Celebrities were tweeting, promoting, and amplifying my article. It created thousands of daily visitors to my website. My DMs on Instagram started blowing up. People were telling me that they had read my coffee blog post and how it inspired them.

This was a piece of content that took me about three hours to create. It could have easily been discarded and offered no return. But, I ran it through a distribution strategy of getting it in front of a larger target audience, and that three-and-a-half hours worth of work led to significant revenue. I frequently update this piece to renew interest and redistribute its ideas. More on redistribution later, but suffice it to say, this piece still generates a lot of traffic, followers, and revenue for me.

And this is a little-known fact, but I also ran a company called Hustle and Grind in 2018, which sold coffee mugs. With some thoughtful content marketing, we sold quite a few mugs, simply from the distributive popularity of my coffee and gangster rap article.

That is the power of distribution: from nothing to revenue. That power is why you should embrace it. In this chapter, you'll learn why embracing distribution now will set you up for long-term success. You should embrace distribution because people are sharing more than before and will continue to share in the future, distribution is more important than the content or product itself, competition is fierce in this noisy world, you likely have the content you need, and real revenue opportunities await.

REASON 1: MORE CONTENT THAN EVER BEFORE

If you don't distribute your work, the abundance of available and soon-to-be-published content will erase the awareness of your valuable content. This is what you're competing with. People share and consume more content than ever before, and you have to compete with that. Embracing a distribution strategy—or even being aware that you need a distribution strategy—can make or break you.

How do we know distribution is powerful in an ocean of content? Many, including myself, view it as more important than the content or product itself. Take finance and tech CEO Alex Rampell, who once famously said, "The battle between every startup and incumbent comes down to whether the startup gets distribution before the incumbent gets innovation."[3] This sounds a little harsh at first glance, but let me explain. Whether we are talking about content

---

3   Alex Rampell, "Distribution vs. Innovation," Andreessen
    Horowitz, November 5, 2015, https://a16z.com/2015/11/05/
    distribution-v-innovation/.

or product, Rampell's point still stands that already-successful companies essentially leverage their distribution to reduce the likelihood of any newcomer entering into their space to disrupt the market. These incumbents can only have competition if their distribution is stripped. Any "innovation" that comes from a startup competitor will simply be used by the incumbent.

Take TikTok as an example. In September of 2022, TikTok added a new feature to allegedly squash burgeoning French social media app BeReal. The new feature, called TikTok Now, functions in nearly the same way as BeReal. The feature invites users to snap photos from the front or back camera at a random time each day. It's not that TikTok is better than BeReal. It's that TikTok already had the distribution, and its ability to generate more revenue rests with its larger audience. So, as Rampell rightly argued, startups need to focus on distribution first prior to innovating. Otherwise, they face their ideas being—the lawyers are advising me to say—borrowed.

The same thing happens with content marketing. Two content marketers can create the exact same words, but one of them has a bigger audience, and the one with the bigger audience is likely to generate more revenue. The other person is left scratching their head and wondering why their amazing content led to nothing.

Distribution itself is an opportunity for revenue generation.

When I talk about the opportunity for revenue expansion offered by distribution, it cannot be overstated that tremendous financial gain is at stake. To demonstrate how, allow me to share an example from my company, Foundation Marketing. In a blog titled, "These SaaS Companies Are Unbundling Excel—Here's Why It's A Massive Opportunity,"[4] I felt I had hit on something important for the business world to see.

Everyone is familiar with Microsoft's Excel. It's a popular program we learn in school. Entire industries operate on the back of Excel. My hypothesis was that there's an opportunity for brands and businesses that utilize Excel to create use cases specific to their industry, such as invoices or CRMs (customer relationship management). Using their use cases, they could develop a niche-specific product because, of course, riches are in the niches. These products could be unbundled from Excel, the way Tinder was an unbundling of the "Missed Connections" of Craigslist.

Once I posted this piece, I linked it in a few Tweets, seeded it on LinkedIn, and uploaded it to Hacker News. Within

---

4   Ross Simmonds, "These SaaS Companies Are Unbundling
     Excel—Here's Why It's a Massive Opportunity,"
     Foundationinc.co, July 22, 2022, https://foundationinc.co/lab/
     the-saas-opportunity-of-unbundling-excel/.

a matter of minutes, it was shared hundreds of times on LinkedIn and thousands of times on Twitter, and it continues to be shared.

I generated eight customer leads within a month. One client, then a stranger, held a brief phone call with me, started briefing me on their company's product, and then shared a $250,000 opportunity worth of business with me. Not a bad outcome for a few hours' work. Create once. Distribute forever.

This type of life-changing money is available to you, too.

You should know that I did this when I was twenty-eight years old. Now I'm much older with a lot more gray hair, but I've reused this single piece of content in a playbook of distribution to generate millions of dollars in business for my company—all by simply embracing basic distribution principles.

If you don't distribute your content consistently and systematically, especially when you're just getting started, you will lose out to those who are louder or have worked to generate a large audience. And the importance of distributing your content surgically to outduel the modern content landscape will only get more important. There's more content, competitors, and distribution than ever before.

Zuckerberg's "Law of Sharing"

The modern content landscape is always changing, but not many recognize how dramatically.

When you create a piece of content, you're making an investment. You want what you've created to have a return. You want it to help people. You want it to drive conversions. You want it to drive sales. You want it to have a positive impact on your business, however that might apply to your situation. The reason? The time that you invest into your content asset is something that will generate an ROI (return on investment). Time and time again, content creators and CEOs are disappointed when their great content marketing is met with silence. Their expectation of its ROI collapses like a flan in a cupboard. How quickly is the landscape changing?

In 2011, while talking at a small conference, Mark Zuckerberg introduced the "Law of Sharing," which is the idea that the amount of online sharing doubles every year. This doubling will continue at that pace for the rest of eternity.

Do a gut check. Think back to 2011 and gauge for yourself. When I reflect on this, it's safe to say there is a lot more online sharing now than there was in 2011. The reason is simple. Millions of us have devices in our pockets that can share anything. You can take photos or even record a video, edit the content, and publish it in a matter of minutes right now.

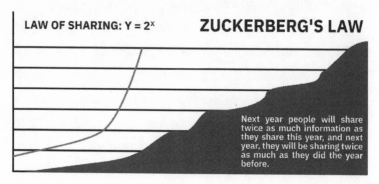

LAW OF SHARING: Y = 2^x **ZUCKERBERG'S LAW**

Next year people will share twice as much information as they share this year, and next year, they will be sharing twice as much as they did the year before.

Figure 2.1

Back in the day, maybe somewhere in the 1990s, if you wanted to create photo content to share, you would need to operate a film camera, wait until the roll ran out, take that film to a local store, wait a few days for the pictures to be developed, return to pick up the pictures, scan them for digitization on your home computer, and then upload them to a website. But not everyone had websites and scanners. What was more likely was sliding the photos into a photobook and sharing that album with the people that visited. So, if it were the 1990s and you had photos you wanted to share, your immediate family might see them around the holidays. Cameras didn't exactly have the distribution they used to, did they?

Now things are different. You can snap a photo of anything and share it with the world instantly. Cats, coffee, food, or this book's cover. You could take a selfie with this book and immediately post that photo to X (formerly known as Twitter), LinkedIn, Instagram, or the social media platform of your choice to show people what you're up to. Do it! I'm serious... I dare you! Take a picture with this book, tag me—@TheCoolestCool—and I would be very grateful for it. More people need to understand the power of distribution, and your share could help one of your friends or peers uncover new opportunities.

The point is that people are sharing and consuming at increasing rates. As more and more people come online, with inventions like satellite internet constellations on the verge of giving universal internet access across the globe, more and more people will be connected to devices. The frequency of online publishing hits all-time highs every year. As a result, brands are up against more noise than ever before when they press publish on a new asset.

Things are noisy. So how do you stand out? You stand out by embracing distribution. Further, as I will detail in Parts 2 and 3, you need to distribute well. You can't assume that publishing something and leaving it in one spot will allow users to happen upon your piece among the sea of stories flooding the internet every single day. There is too much competition.

REASON 2: MORE COMPETITION THAN BEFORE

Embrace distribution because you are competing with more creators than ever before. It's easier than ever to create software, build a following online, and launch a small business or start a freelance company. Creating a business in general has never been easier. There are multiple reasons why. First, as generations that grew up with modern technology enter the working world, their skills translate easily to the age of content. But also, barriers to entering the entrepreneur's or a creator's worlds are at an all-time low. Give someone a bit of wifi, good coffee, and a vision, and they can build something special from a laptop or phone.

In the past, it was expensive to launch a software company or create an amazing piece of content. There used to be lots of specialty equipment that, because of their niche functions, required a range of professionals. Now, anybody can use a phone to write a blog post, record a podcast, or shoot a video and then edit it to professional quality and post it to their desired distribution channels—all within that same device.

In 2011, there were around 150 marketing technology (martech) companies in existence. Today, that number has ballooned to more than 9,500 companies. No need to pull out your calculator, I'll do the math for you. That's a 6,233-percent increase. The number of total martech companies will only continue to grow as technology keeps changing. This rise in new businesses, new technologies, and new innovation is what you're competing with.

Here's something else that you're competing with: the teen up the street. A recent survey found that 54 percent of Americans aged thirteen to thirty-eight want to become a social media influencer.[5] In that same study, 30 percent of kids in the UK listed "YouTuber" as their top career choice. Whether you love it or hate it—the world wants to create. And content creation and its importance are only going to continue to grow and become more prevalent as time goes on.

Because of this surge in the creator economy, you again are up against a plethora of people looking to capture the attention of your ideal audience. And, as I discussed earlier, it doesn't necessarily matter how strong or weak your competitors' content or products might be. Their ability to distribute supersedes the content, in many ways. Marc Andreessen, the Co-Founder of Andreessen Horowitz, a VC firm that invested in a few startups that knew a lot

---

5   Baz Macdonald, "54% of Young People Want to Be Social Media Influencers—Is It a Bad Thing?" 1News, September 29, 2022, https://www.1news.co.nz/2022/09/29/54-of-young-people-want-to-be-influencers-is-it-a-bad-thing/.

about distribution—like Stripe, Instacart, Databricks, and OpenSea—summed it up this way: "The general model for successful tech companies, contrary to myth and legend, is that they become distribution-centric rather than product-centric."[6]

Every day, people are getting emails from people all over the world, asking them to check out a demo, a product, read a piece of content, or give them feedback on something. You are competing with all of that. As every day passes, more and more competition is actively and intentionally going after your audience.

Promoting your company and distributing your content becomes the necessary tool to set yourself apart. So you need to not only embrace the process but think about *how* to distribute it. You can't just press "publish" and wait. Don't forget the revenue expansion at stake. You have to publish and then be aggressive, if not relentless, at spreading your stories and getting your content in front of the right people.

In total, and because there is so much to compete with, you need to ensure two things:

6   Elad Gil. "Where to Go After Product-Market Fit: An Interview with Marc Andreessen," Future.com, July 20, 2018, https://future.com/go-product-market-fit-interview-marc-andreessen/.

1. That you're producing and creating high-value content, and
2. You're distributing in channels where your audience is spending time.

Don't worry. I'll be showing you how to do and think about both of these later on.

REASON 3: MORE DISTRIBUTION CHANNELS THAN BEFORE

Embracing distribution is crucial because of the multiple opportunities offered by the vast array of modern channels. In the early 2000s, there were limited social media platforms and forums like Reddit, Facebook, X (formerly known as Twitter), and LinkedIn. However, technological advances have resulted in the emergence of Slack, Discord, Instagram, Twitch, TikTok, and many more.

Each of these newer platforms has steadily garnered the prolonged attention of audiences. As audiences spend their time on more and more platforms, user attention spreads to the many channels and away from the previously few options. Market trends indicate that users will continue to spread onto new platforms.

Every single year, a new channel pops up that captures the attention and minds of millions of people. The increasing number of social networks has also made it more important for us to invest in distribution not just because the channels exist, mind you, but because these channels are capturing more and more of your target consumer's time. You will need to evolve your strategy with your evolving audience.

"Channel" may be an odd word to use, especially for folks over thirty. But TV channels are out, online channels are in. Less and less time is being spent sitting in front of a TV and more and more time is spent on new, online channels, such as TikTok, Snapchat, LinkedIn, Instagram, and any number of others that have become popular since this book's publication.

Where there is attention, there is opportunity. Make it a point to understand channels and the people spending their time there. So, another answer to the question "Why should I embrace distribution?" is prompted by audience dilution across many channels. With audience dilution part of the challenge, you have to extend your content tentacles beyond a single distribution channel while also adopting a choreographed distribution playbook—but more on that later.

REASON 4: MORE OPPORTUNITY THAN BEFORE

It's easy to be overwhelmed by everything standing in your way. With each passing moment, there is more competition, more content, more cat photos, more memes, and more everything than ever. How are you going to navigate the complexities of distribution and succeed? By understanding that the opportunity outweighs the difficulty. Embracing distribution means life-changing revenue opportunities.

If you're willing to put in the work and compete with brands willing to get scrappier than you, you can use a think-quick strategy to distribute your content that takes full advantage of distribution channels. You will be focused on navigating international distribution in ways that you have not in the past.

We live in a global world. Your audience is bigger than you might realize. Think about how your life may change if you adopt distribution. In fact, I like to imagine how distribution might change the life of a person with an "ordinary," non-tech job to demonstrate distribution's importance.

Let's imagine the life of a locksmith. Mere decades ago, a locksmith could only distribute to the people who lived in their local, surrounding area. They built their business around a service many found value in. Those in their city or district were the total customer pool. Perhaps the customers were primarily builders and local residents wanting new locks or keys.

But today, thanks to online distribution channels, that locksmith could offer their services and content on a global level. They could produce how-to videos on YouTube or buying guides on Instagram to spread their story even further. Let's say they wanted to connect with interior designers who then act as a reseller of their lockmanship in many ways. At the time of writing, there is a Facebook Group called Interior Designers with over 478,000 members. By offering products online and creating content that resonates with interior designers this locksmith could grow their sales by distributing their story in this Group. The truth is that the potential audience for this locksmith is bigger than ever.

A sports coach need not be relegated to coaching one team in their neighborhood, thanks to YouTube. A make-up artist need not beautify just the person sitting in their chair, thanks to Patreon. Name any occupation, and there are vast distribution channels waiting to help scale and reach more people.

I am living proof of this growth. As mentioned, I live in Nova Scotia, and not many have heard of this relatively remote area, unless it was from a movie about fishing or rural Canadian life. Yet, I'm able to create content for millions of people and work with the CEOs of billion-dollar companies.

Not only is your reach long regardless of your place, but your ideal audience tends to spend their time in specific corners of the internet. That means you don't have to cast an impossibly wide net. Instead, you can precisely target your distribution to serve specific groups, even redistributing content that didn't generate traction the first time around. When you do distribute, you can overcome the modern market difficulties of more channels, more competitors, and more noise.

Just think of your possible audience pool. Take Facebook Groups. Every month, there are 1.8 billion people who use Facebook Groups. These groups are filled with people who have interests in all kinds of wide-ranging topics—things like interior design, machine learning, sales, marketing technology, the Philadelphia Eagles (Go Birds!), and BBQ, to name a few.

A nearly two-billion-person audience is available to you with just one feature of one social media platform. As the book continues, we'll cover all of the major online channels. So, if you do not believe your audience is online, I challenge you to see if there's a group or forum that exists where your audience is spending time. And I can say this with confidence: these are audience forums where you should be thinking about how you can capitalize on distributing your content.

Distribution is your best opportunity to realize the vision and dreams for your product, service, or content at large. Embrace it. As LinkedIn co-founder Reid Hoffman once remarked, "Product distribution is more important than product."[7]

DON'T UNDERESTIMATE YOUR VALUE

When I look around, I notice that many creators, founders, or content marketers hold themselves back from distributing their work because they underestimate the value of something they've created in the past. To these folks I say this: remember that the one day you decide to share your work, be it three days, three weeks, or three months ago, your audience just might not have been there that day. So, just because it didn't get traction doesn't mean that it did not have potential and that you should call it quits.

Remember my own initial "failure" with my piece about coffee and hip-hop. It was met with crickets the first time I shared it. It wasn't until I put it through a carefully thought-out distribution engine that it reified into something widely read.

Don't be afraid to repromote something you have previously published that didn't get any traction. Too often, that first iteration's lack of success is used as an indicator that

---

7   Josh Elman, "Reid Hoffman Fireside with Josh Elan," Boomplay, December 6, 2016, https://www.boomplay.com/episode/1864646/.

there is something wrong with the content itself. However, non-engagement is more likely a signal that the content actually needs a better distribution strategy.

Yes, there are challenges. There are more channels and more content than ever before. But there are also more people online than ever. And where there is challenge, there is tremendous opportunity. You should focus on the potential in front of you. You could fundamentally change your life by simply taking an asset that you've created in the past and spreading it online to the right people in the right channels at the right time.

My essay about Excel and SaaS has generated me hundreds of thousands of dollars in revenue. Other blog posts that we distributed about brands like Canva, Masterclass, Salesforce, and more have earned millions. And guess what? As you're reading this, our team has probably reshared all of the above somewhere on the internet within the last week, and it will continue to reap benefits. We created these pieces of content once, but we will distribute them forever as they continue to ring the cash register for hundreds of thousands of dollars each month in sales. Amplifying your content means overcoming the mistake of not believing your content is worth sharing.

I want to give you more space to acknowledge the possible apprehensions you feel. It is normal to resist self-promotion. Distributing content can feel like one is selling themselves at times. I hear you. That's a valid feeling. But you need to overcome some of those mental roadblocks that are holding you back.

On the other end of those roadblocks is a dream life you could have only imagined. In order to free up the path to that dream, I'll move next to discussing the typical reasons people don't embrace distribution. With those reasons identified, we can move beyond them to unlock the power of distribution.

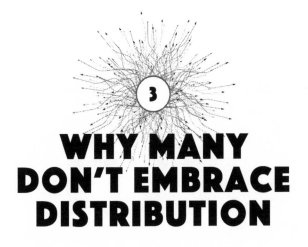

WHY MANY
DON'T EMBRACE
DISTRIBUTION

ISTRIBUTION ISN'T EASY. I SAY THAT FROM PER-
sonal experience, summed up in my earliest forays
with Reddit.

Reddit is a channel that most marketers are afraid
of, and for good reasons. If you act like a marketer spamming Reddit, you will get banned, and the community will
tell you where to go and how to get there.

I consider myself a Redditor first and a marketer second.
Despite that, I've been banned from the platform more

than four times, but I've come back and now understand how to make the front page with relative ease.

But let me take you back in time to the earliest days of my Reddit usage. As a new r/technology user, I wasn't entirely familiar with its rules. I sought to distribute a piece of content I had written about marketing tech, so I submitted it under the tech subreddit (specific communities within Reddit). Thinking more is better, I also submitted it to the machine learning, algorithms, marketing, business, and software engineering subreddits. Within a matter of five minutes, my account was blocked and banned. For the Reddit community, those actions were considered spamming. They shut me down and told me I was done with Reddit permanently. Bye, Felicia. You're out of here. It was painful.

I could have given up and said, "All right, I guess I can't distribute my content on Reddit." Instead, I decided I was going to use this as a learning opportunity to understand how I could thrive on Reddit. How could I distribute on this heavily used channel while abiding by the rules? So I studied the rules. Next was learning from the best content on Reddit. Before long, and after creating new accounts, I was able to post content that made Reddit's front page and helped me reach millions.

Although what I did with Reddit is accomplishable with any platform, I need to reiterate a valuable lesson: each distribution channel has its own rules and conventions that are not limitations but rather gateways to distribution success.

Today, I can say with confidence that I can get on the front page of Reddit within a matter of minutes. I know the code. I've been on the front page of Reddit two or three dozen times all through content tailored to the target Redditor's wants and needs.

The only way anybody can succeed on Reddit is by studying the channel, becoming immersed in the subreddits their audience uses, and enduring a few lumps along the way. I see it time and time again with marketers, businesses, and entrepreneurs that test the waters of Reddit. They start submitting a bunch of links to subreddits, hoping they'll be successful. Instead, they are met with the big "blocked" sign.

But why endure constant lumps and headaches when you can learn it from someone else? My hope for you is that this book helps you avoid having to learn the hard way. I don't want you to get blocked on Reddit. I don't want you to be met with crickets when you launch. I don't want you to have content fall flat. I want you to win. So, by learning how to distribute your content the right way, you will unlock new levels of growth and ensure your stories spread like wildfire.

So often, I see marketers let the first flop stop them from continuing to distribute content, which is what we'll cover in this chapter. You have likely felt or are about to feel many of these roadblocks, and I want to address them for you. Let's get them out in the open—name the beast to tame the beast, as they say. Three major reasons people don't embrace distribution are fear of doing it poorly, a perceived lack of expertise, and giving up before seeing success. We will cover these and several other mindset-related obstacles standing in the way of marketers.

Overcome them, and you will unlock the opportunities of distribution.

THE FEARS HOLDING YOU BACK FROM DISTRIBUTION

Every creative has two dilemmas. You can be someone who creates, waits, and hopes that good things are going to happen to you. Or you can be the person who creates and distributes deliberately. Every day, many creators take the first, luck-based path. Eventually, they quit before realizing their full potential. Either they are ashamed to promote themselves, afraid that they'll fail, or any other number of fears that stop them from breaking through their own limits. Creators with these issues will tend to be the "hope for the best" or "blame the system" instead of taking their fate into their own hands. If you've fallen into that mindset trap, I'm here to help you snap out of it.

Let's conduct a thought experiment. Imagine an under-rated, underground, and unknown musician who produces excellent music that you (and all your friends) would love. The musician isn't willing to go on tour. Perhaps they have too much fear to play in front of a crowd or too much ego to play in small arenas and get their foot in the proverbial door. Maybe they don't want to share tour dates on their social media because they don't want to seem "too promotional." And they don't want to email their friends or colleagues about their latest music, all because of fear of technology. The end result is a great musician whose excellent music is not heard by you or anybody. The musician's mindset holds back themselves and would-be listeners of something spe-cial. And it's possible that you've done something similar.

This mindset is a waste of talent and arguably life. If you believe in the work you've created, then you should feel good and excited to distribute it as well as you can. Otherwise, you're doing your audience a disservice by not distributing something that would benefit them. Helping your audience find value is not selling out. This is not only about you. It's about helping other people who are strug-gling with the thing you can help them with. It's time to get over your fears.

CREATE ONCE, DISTRIBUTE FOREVER

The Fear of Being Unfollowed

There are a lot of reasons to be afraid of distribution. Perhaps the most emotionally painful fear is that of losing social validation with your peers by coming off as too promotional or, as some would describe it, selling out.

To be fair, there's a real horror movie called *Unfollowed*, and it's not meant as a joke. Social fear is a genuine fear.

Social invalidation comes in many forms, though, not just being unfollowed. It could also manifest as a fear of negative comments or the idea that people will mute your account without you even realizing it. These interactions, to some, can feel like personal attacks. There is something about our wiring as humans that deeply cares about how others view us.

So, how can we overcome this fear? By internalizing one simple truth about the internet: In reality, no one really cares that much. And if they do unfollow you, mute your account, or block you on social media, does it really matter? You can't pay the bills with opinions. It's not likely they were going to help pay your bills down the road anyway. If someone doesn't like your content, ninety-nine times out of a hundred, they will scroll past it.

Thousands of people scrolling past your work is not an indicator that your content is bad. It's likely that at that moment they simply were not your target audience and what you shared may not have caught their attention. The vast majority of people who see the link or headline to your content will choose not to engage—and that's okay. When it comes to distribution, if you pull even 10 percent engagement, you are considered wildly successful. This can sometimes be something hard to wrap your head around because if you received a 10 percent on an exam, for example, you "failed." It's important to remember that success and failure are relative. Turning 5,000 website visits into one client, or some such "poor" ratio, could very well mean game-changing money for you or your business.

You have to get over your fear of what others may say or think about you or your brand. As the popular saying goes, "Haters are gonna hate." As you grow comfortable with distributing your content, a new group of like-minded and open-minded people will start following and flocking toward you. This is the audience we focus on. Do not fear the haters.

The Fear of Being an Imposter

Imposter Syndrome is a psychological phenomenon wherein an individual doubts their abilities and feels like a fraud despite evidence of their accomplishments. This mindset can be particularly debilitating for individuals looking to promote their content online. Confidence in content can lapse. They may feel like their work isn't "good enough" or that they don't deserve their success, causing them to shy away from promoting themselves.

The fear of being exposed as a fraud can hold people back, resulting in missed opportunities for exposure and growth. Even if someone has a significant following, they may still struggle to feel like they belong in their position, leading to self-doubt and second-guessing. Tom Hanks even suffered from Imposter Syndrome: "No matter what we've done, there comes a point where you think, 'How did I get here? When are they going to discover that I am, in fact, a fraud and take everything away from me?'"

Furthermore, individuals with Imposter Syndrome may struggle to take constructive criticism, feeling as if any feedback they receive is proof that they're not good enough. This can hinder their growth and progress toward goals.

Overall, Imposter Syndrome can be a significant hurdle for individuals looking to promote their content online. It's essential to recognize when these feelings arise and take steps to push past them. Do so by surrounding yourself with supportive individuals, celebrating small wins, and reframing negative self-talk into positive self-talk.

The Fear of Experimentation

Every year, I like to experiment with a new channel. It's a personal challenge to figure out how to crack the code as it relates to a new social network, technology, or community. One year it was SlideShare. Another, Quora. Afterward, I make it a point to create a piece of content to summarize the findings and lessons learned. Many of those kinds of lessons will appear in Part 3.

You never know when your experimentation will lead to a new insight, a new distribution opportunity, or a moment when you strike gold. For example, after learning Quora, the "here are my findings" piece of content I created landed me in Forbes magazine multiple times with stories about Jay-Z and Rockstar Games that generated millions of reads.

If you keep yourself open, experiment with new possibilities, and move past the initial challenge of not knowing what you're doing, you can go far. Yes, you might not be successful at first. But the more you experiment, the more insight you glean on how to effectively distribute your content.

The Fear of Time Commitment

Some people hold the view that distribution efforts and the initial learning curve upfront take too much time. It is true that it is a lot of work. However, it is not true that it takes *too* much time. In fact, in the long run, your returns will grow while your hours will remain constant (and sometimes lessen).

How can your growth scale? Let's look at two possible scenarios. First scenario: You could spend time generating many pieces of great content, thinking that content is most important. You hit "publish" on these pieces of content and only receive a small amount of total engagement before moving on to the next creation piece. Total time invested is two to four hours.

Second scenario: You could spend an equal amount of time creating one piece of content, consider how to distribute it well, distribute it, and generate even more engagement and returns than you would if you just hit publish.

Yes, the time invested is greater, but the return from the initial investment in creating is greater—ideally, more than two times greater because you have embraced a distribution strategy that allowed you to reach more than twenty times the amount of people you would have seen if you just hit publish. More often than not, the biggest mistake that people and brands make is that they overestimate the importance of production and underestimate the importance of distribution. The time you would have spent creating the next piece can be allocated to promoting the last piece.

If you're a founder or an entrepreneur, you probably don't have a lot of time. You may believe in the importance of distribution but aren't sure how to fit it into the schedule.

I'm here to tell you—although they will be covered in more detail later—there are ways you can become more efficient in your distribution channels.

One of those time-saving strategies is to schedule your distribution ahead of time. While you are reading this chapter, I've probably sent out about six Tweets, posted two LinkedIn articles, and shared something on Instagram. I use tools to schedule my content in advance, and you can do the same. In fact, I have a Tweet scheduled for 2089, and it's going to say "Kids, I miss you and love you." Please don't ruin the surprise for them. (If you are my kid and bought my book to support me, this is possibly the worst spoiler alert of all time. I'm hoping you forget by the time 2089 rolls around.) Either way, this tweet will be fulfilling because, while I won't be around physically, I will still be able to tell my kids how much they mean to me.

A lot of people underestimate the power of scheduling things to get ahead on distribution. It's even useful for obligatory social media posts on anniversaries, birthdays, and Valentine's Day, to avoid the dog house.

There is no better tool for busy people than content schedulers. Go to Google and find a content scheduling tool that works for you and the distribution channels you use.

The Fear of Being Judged

Not always, but sometimes, creators overestimate their reach and influence. Harsh truth. In most cases, your audience is much smaller than you actually think, and to avoid this misguided thinking you should be promoting your work daily. Don't make the mistake of thinking you're above distribution. Everybody thinks they are a good driver despite the impossibility of everyone on the road being a good driver, right? Or am I the only one with a family member who thinks they are a terrific driver despite me gripping the grab handle tightly the entire ride?

Most people think they are amazing, and that is also true when it comes to sharing things online. Somebody posts to LinkedIn, gets a few likes, and believes droves of users have possibly clicked on and read the content. One like means a hundred people have read it, right? Wrong. The truth is, we humans are apt to get caught up in our own ego a little bit. Even those few people who liked the post probably didn't make it past the headline.

Don't carry delusions of grandeur. Even Beyonce has to promote her albums. If you are bigger than Beyonce, then well done. But, let's face it, you're not. But if somehow you are, then I'm thrilled you found my book, and I encourage you to tweet about how you're reading these words. Okay. Back to regularly scheduled programming.

Don't overestimate your reach or underestimate how your ego could be holding you back. Promote your work. Distribute your stories. And remember there are millions of people out there who haven't heard of you yet because you're not willing to put yourself out there.

OPPORTUNITIES, NOT OBSTACLES

When it comes to distribution, it really takes a lot of self-work. You have to figure out what you want to do deep down. Why is it that you are not willing to promote your creations? We all have a limited amount of time in this world, and you probably spent a good chunk of it creating something valuable. Lo and behold, your audience spends a lot of time searching their online channels to experience and consume the things you offer. Why not take the opportunity to bridge these two experiences by distributing your content?

My hope is that you are able to escape any mental road-blocks preventing you from distributing your asset, your product, or your content. Put in the work. Ask the tough questions, look inward, and fortify yourself. "Why do I care so much about what people think of my content?" "Why am I so afraid of learning something new?"

In a week, nobody is going to care about what you posted today. The most viral story making headlines today will be long forgotten when something else has the world's attention. The same thinking needs to be applied to your distribution efforts. Promote your work.

HOW AND WHERE
TO DISTRIBUTE
CONTENT

O NE OF THE MOST INFLUENTIAL LITERARY CHARAC-
ters in my life is Sherlock Holmes. With your permis-
sion, I'd like to nerd-out about him a little bit.

During a given case, Holmes had this uncanny
ability to tap into his "brain attic," as Arthur Conan Doyle
described it. There, Holmes would use his stellar mem-
ory and deductive reasoning to piece together and solve a
mystery. But when he used these skills, he didn't do so in a
vacuum. He relied on data.

In "The Adventure of the Speckled Band," Holmes specifically cites his need for data to aid in decision-making, shouting, "Data! Data! Data!... I can't make bricks without clay."[8] During this same rant, Holmes comments on the dangers of not having enough of it: "'I had,' [Holmes] said, 'come to an entirely erroneous conclusion which shows, my dear Watson, how dangerous it always is to reason from insufficient data." This isn't the only instance where Holmes states the importance of reliable data.

Forms of Holmes' data-keeping strategy emerge throughout the series. In the very first Sherlock Holmes novel, 1887's *A Study in Scarlet*, Holmes notices the ash from a Trichnopoly cigar at the crime scene. Thankfully, his data-filled monograph on the subject of cigars helps him solve the case. In three other stories, his monograph on cigar ashes continues to aid his work in solving the respective mysteries. Elsewhere, in "A Case of Identity," Holmes finds files on his past experience with typewriters that note how each machine has its own peculiarities. That knowledge helps him solve the case.

What can we glean from this? Each Holmes story follows the same formula. He's unable to solve the mystery, so

---

8   Arthur Conan Doyle, *The Adventures of Sherlock Holmes* (New York, Dover Publications: 2009), 150.

he collects data and looks at patterns in past occurrences to get closer and closer until, near the end of the story, he makes the right choice.

It is often difficult for companies, brands, and creators to identify in their brain attic where they should be distributing their content. There are many different options when trying to solve that particular mystery. Where should they publish? What's to be done after publishing? These kinds of choices can be intimidating.

To solve this mystery, I encourage you to put on your Sherlock Holmes hat and dive deep into data to understand and identify where your audience is by spending the time. Doing so will familiarize you with the channels they use and illuminate how they're consuming content on said channels. Having this data will help you more precisely tailor your content and your content's distribution.

As much as I love Sherlock Holmes, I'm not him. But I wanted to blend his approach to solving mysteries with my own approach to finding distribution channels worth embracing. Flash forward to a marketing conference, and I called myself "Sherlock Homeboy" when describing the idea of reverse-engineering marketing channels. When you put on our Sherlock Homeboy hat, you need to put yourself into the mind of the person you're trying to connect with—your target audience.

Throughout this chapter, I will walk you through the process that I embrace to better understand my audience and their channels. With the Sherlock Homeboy Method mastered, anyone can ensure that their asset, product, or piece of content spreads effectively.

THE SHERLOCK HOMEBOY METHOD

Don't assume that you know where your audience is spending their time. You shouldn't use your gut instinct or anecdotal experience to make a judgment on their channel habits. Instead, you should steal the strategies of those who have already found success on different channels. Collect and reverse-engineer that data to unlock success with your own approach. Picasso once said that great artists don't copy, they steal. Marketers should do the same.

How does the Sherlock Homeboy Method work? Let's say a company notices data suggesting their audience has expressed a keen interest in consuming vertical video content from YouTube and TikTok. But, a caveat is that their audience does this on personal time without a direct bearing on their professional roles. Perhaps, though, there is an opportunity to start giving them professional content on this channel. They could borrow the concept of vertical video and apply the organization's mission and message. By stealing—I mean leveraging—a new channel, the company has unlocked value using a data-backed strategy.

The idea of the Sherlock Homeboy Method is to reverse-engineer information for the purpose of utilizing opportunities for success. In order to reverse-engineer, you first need information. So, what are the crucial things you need to investigate?

UNLOCKING CHANNEL-USER FIT

The first thing you need to do is figure out where your audience is spending time online. I like to call this channel-user fit, defined as the channels in which your ideal customers, users, or audience are spending time online. It makes no sense for a brand to go to a random channel and distribute content to a random audience. There is a strong chance the audience doesn't need or want what you are offering. That would be like going to an uninhabited desert and trying to sell cold bottles of water.

The Sherlock Homeboy Method allows you to discover the channels of your target audience and whether or not your asset can be successfully distributed there. These are a few investigatory steps to take to find channel-user fit.

Step 1: Talk to Your Audience

You likely have customers who could act as proxies of your average customer persona or ideal customer. Talk to them. The essence of what you're trying to accomplish is to get to know your audience, so get to know them.

Ask them what channels they spend their time on, for what reasons, and how much time they spend logged onto those channels. Which channels do they go to for shop-talk and which only for recreational purposes? These are things you want to figure out, as they will inform your distribution strategy. You may decide not to intrude on the channels your customer goes to in order to escape.

Step 2: Find Core Distribution Channels

While your ideal audience may be diluted across multiple distribution channels, you can identify their core channels by validating their usage in top channels. To get started, peruse the top channels for distribution, such as Facebook, LinkedIn, Twitter, and Instagram. Locate your competitors' sub-channels within these to validate core channels of your audience. Also, do some research about the core channels where conversations about your content subject occur.

What core channels apply to your audience search will depend entirely on the nature of your content or product. For example, if you are a software-as-a-service company in the sales software space, you would easily find your audience spending time on LinkedIn. Let's say an indirect competitor sells AI that helps sales teams better understand how their calls are going across the org and has a massive LinkedIn presence. A quick, reverse-engineered look at this brand's online distribution would show insights that validate that this channel is aligned with your targets. All of this information confirms that the core channel you should be distributing on is LinkedIn.

If you are finding it difficult to pin down your audience's location, consider using audience analytics tools. Companies like Audiense, SparkToro, Moz, Semrush, or Ahrefs all provide data that can help you better understand your audience, down to the keywords they type into Google and podcasts they follow online.

UNLOCKING CONTENT-USER FIT

After you find your audience's distribution channels, there are several metrics you should look for to understand what content your audience loves on these channels. A starting metric is how many subscribers the Facebook Group, Instagram hashtag, or Twitter account has. Obviously, you want to go into the channels with the largest audience to ensure you can reach the most people.

Next, what types of posts generate a lot of engagement? What topics, stories, and structures resonate with your ideal customers the most? Maybe that means posts with the most likes, upvotes, or comments. The metric will depend on the channel and what's important to your content. Knowing what content is most popular gives you a framework by which to model your own. As is the thesis of the Sherlock Homeboy Method, this content can be reverse-engineered for your purposes.

It's possible your audience is present in a distribution channel but does not engage with content. This can happen for several reasons. It might be the platform has a pay-to-play business model that drives down freely or organically posted material. At the time of writing, these platforms are experiencing a 5.2 percent reach, meaning that only one out of every nineteen people will come upon content organically. The other eighteen are experiencing content that was paid for.

Of course, you can find data insights that suggest the estimated engagement rate of any channel. However, manually checking these channels to see the type of content that drives engagement is also a valuable practice.

Review Competitor Content

We have touched on competitors a bit so far, but there are several things you can do with competitor presence to help you understand and find your audience. To what extent is your competition distributing in a certain channel? Factors to consider include the total number of competitors as well as the breadth of their content.

Closely examine their content. What about their publications seems to be working for them? What could be improved? They've tailored their content to your mutual audience. Steal their approach while adding your own tweaks and improvements.

One of my favorite things to do is go into a subreddit where I know my audience is spending time and sort the content by top posts. By doing so, I'm able to see what the best competitor posts are in the subreddit. My competitor's posts are wonderful templates for creating engagement for my own content. Find out what your competition does and where they do it. After reverse-engineering it, do it better.

You should also consider whether or not your competitor takes a similar or different market position or voice to your brand. How do their nuanced differences or similarities impact the audience's engagement?

In some cases, you might be the first to arrive at a distribution channel. It's competitor-less! If you are early, there is good news and bad news. The good news is that, as the first one in the door, you have first dibs at the untapped potential of the channel. The bad news is that you won't be able to look at your competitors to discern whether or not it's a viable channel. However, you can compare this new channel to the channels your competitors do publish on to make a calculated risk.

Uncover Content-Market Fit

Now let's talk about delivering consistent value to your audience. You should now have a better idea of where your audience is (channel-user fit) and what type of content they prefer consuming (content-user fit). By meeting them on their terms, it means ensuring the content you distribute is of high value to them. At this point, you can abandon or avoid the "spray and pray" approach of distributing lots of mediocre content in all channels. Instead, you can adopt a strategy where all of your resources are focused on distributing content tailored to the expectations of what quality means for that channel and your audience.

For example, let's say I'm a psychologist who specializes in sleep training for toddlers and I have courses, books, training, and more ready to sell. There are currently thousands of parents inside Facebook groups learning how to implement sleep training for their children (channel-user fit). If the psychologist has content about sleep training in the form of YouTube videos, blog posts, and TikTok videos on these topics (content-user fit), they can promote some of that content into a Facebook group and generate ridiculous traction from desperate parents looking for one decent night's sleep. This is content-market fit. This is the method I've applied in Facebook Groups to generate revenue for Foundation. It's the method I've used to generate revenue for clients. And it's the method I want you to use to be ridiculously successful.

Test and Adjust Your Content-Market Fit

Testing your content idea on a distribution channel is a great way of determining how the content, channel, and audience are aligned. As you test, collect data, and reiterate, your content will hopefully become more aligned with your new understanding of your audience, helping your content take off on that channel.

The first step is to identify the metrics that will tell you whether or not the asset is successful. For example, are you looking for Reddit upvotes, comments on LinkedIn, or referral traffic from Facebook? The metrics applicable to your asset depend on your unique situation, goals, and objectives. Let's say a person sends out a tweet that generates 109 retweets, 15 quote tweets, and 412 likes. While this may prove that the audience on X/Twitter wants this content, it can also prove they don't want it. How? The quality of engagement. A ton of likes and comments may not mean much if they aren't coming from your ideal customers. That means the content and audience are not aligned.

And even when the content is retweeted or shared by your audience, you need to check out why this happens. Are they agreeing with the content? Are they subtweeting and saying it's bad advice? Check out all of the meaningful engagements, and you'll know if there is more to discover about your audience or how to tailor your content.

Putting It All Together—Content-Market Fit

To summarize, all of the steps of the Sherlock Homeboy Method I've just covered occur over three general phases. The first identifies the audience channels. Second, you determine the content your audience wants most, and, in phase three, you remix or adjust your content and measure reaction. Here is how it might look, graphed in such a manner that may or may not apply to your specific situation.

When you talk to your audience and find core distribution channels, you are determining what I call channel-user fit. That's your channel and audience-finding component.

Once you've discovered the channels you want to meet your audience in, then you need to determine content-user fit. In other words, discover how to adjust your content to fit your audience's narrative expectation of a given channel. To reverse-engineer the content user-fit, examine user

HOW TO UNCOVER CONTENT-MARKET FIT (THE FRAMEWORK)
The Three-Step Process For Ideation, Discovery, and Differentiation

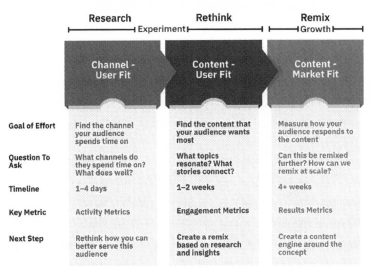

	Research	Rethink	Remix
	Channel - User Fit	Content - User Fit	Content - Market Fit
Goal of Effort	Find the channel your audience spends time on	Find the content that your audience wants most	Measure how your audience responds to the content
Question To Ask	What channels do they spend time on? What does well?	What topics resonate? What stories connect?	Can this be remixed further? How can we remix at scale?
Timeline	1–4 days	1–2 weeks	4+ weeks
Key Metric	Activity Metrics	Engagement Metrics	Results Metrics
Next Step	Rethink how you can better serve this audience	Create a remix based on research and insights	Create a content engine around the concept

Figure 4.1

engagement as well as study competitors to see what has worked best in the past.

Finally, to create content-market fit—or to optimize your audience's engagement with your content—that's when you gauge a channel's reach, create content precisely for a specific channel, and test a publication. With enough data-backed experimentation and adjustment, you will find a strong distribution strategy, one reverse-engineered by the Sherlock Homeboy Method.

If all goes well, you will have hit that eureka moment where you know exactly what type of content resonates with your target audience. The only thing left to do is to repurpose and distribute your content in a scalable way.

Through a combination of qualitative and quantitative research, move yourself from channel-user fit to content-user fit before finally reaching content-market fit. Embrace your own inner Sherlock Homeboy. Once you arrive at content-market fit, a distribution channel is yours for the taking.

Continue to keep your Sherlock Homeboy hat on, though, and consistently look for metrics and responses from your audience in order to make any necessary changes as platforms and channels evolve. Further, remix content into new mediums. One blog post can turn into countless remixed pieces of content that create content-market fit and keep your audience engaged with your materials. Your goal should be to distribute forever.

THE DISTRIBUTION CHANNEL MATRIX

The Sherlock Homeboy Method results in a high likelihood of success for your work. But there is good distribution and great distribution. When you can consistently drive results from a channel, you have good distribution. It might be expensive. It might take time. It might even have lots of competition. But you know it's going to work. Great distribution is when you can consistently drive results from a channel that your competition has overlooked or cannot access. Strive for great distribution.

These two types of distribution make up the top two quadrants of Foundation Marketing's Distribution Matrix.

THE CHANNEL DISTRIBUTION FRAMEWORK
B2B SAAS EXAMPLE

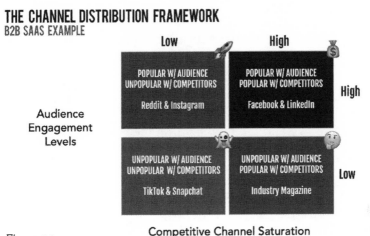

Figure 4.2

The best approach you can take in determining which channels are best for your content is to identify both those opportunities that are popular with your audience as well as your competition. Those channels will (nearly) always be a cash cow. They will consistently generate traffic and results. But, you also want to keep your finger on the pulse of rare channels that may be popular with your audience and unpopular with your competitors.

This distribution channel matrix is a high-level overview of how I think about content distribution. Within this matrix are four distribution channels, each with its own advantages and disadvantages.

Rocket Channels

These are channels that your ideal audience spends their time in. However, your competition has written this channel off for whatever reason. It may be that a software company presents itself as overly professional and has written off the dance videos in TikTok as beneath its brand. Therefore, they willfully ignore that their ideal customer is spending a large chunk of their week on TikTok. That's your cue to jump in and take advantage. Think about industry-leading brands, like Adobe, who have started to create content for TikTok to rocket engagement. It was a smart move for Adobe. They already have a very large market share for creativity apps. By making their presence known in TikTok, they ensure that any competitors stand less of a chance of cutting into that audience.

Rocket channels can be risky because the known branding of a product or content may not translate well in the conventions or rules of the channel, and producing content at scale for these platforms is an uphill battle. It will take quite a bit of marketing work to remix the brand in a way

HOW AND WHERE TO DISTRIBUTE CONTENT

that resonates with users. Other barriers could be regulatory or directly related to access in the form of partners or marketplaces.

Some people will write off rocket channels because they personally don't use them. Think of the uncle at the family get-together who derides this new fandangled such-and-such social media platform. "I just don't understand it," he grimaces while his nieces and nephews smirk. Personal bias often comes into the mix, and a decision-maker might assume that because they don't use a given platform, their audience doesn't either. Of course, that decision-making process is often unsound. And no decision-maker should rely on bias to make an important business decision.

In the end, rocket channels give you an opportunity for unprecedented growth. They can rocket you to the moon.

Money Channels

Money channels should make you money. It's that simple. These are validated channels that are already generating results for your competitors and maybe even you. Both your audience and your competition use them frequently. Your chance of success with these channels is high because your competition has proven that your audience resides here. There is nothing more competitive than a money channel, but there's also nothing as consistently lucrative.

Here are a few examples of audiences, industries, and the money channels that exist:

Industry	Audience	Channel
Software	B2B Sales Professionals	LinkedIn
Software	Technologists	Twitter
Services	Small Business Owners	Meta Properties
Real Estate	Real Estate Buyers	Instagram
Tourism	Young Travelers	TikTok

Use money channels to find a more targeted distribution.

One small warning. Recognize that these channels won't exist forever. The channel that is printing money today might dry up in the future. A big mistake that many brands make is putting all of their efforts into money channels, setting it, and forgetting it. Be mindful when investing in money channels, as the future is unpredictable. Your investment in these channels does not mean you should allow the past to cloud your vision and stop you from consistently reassessing their value to your goals. Think of all of the companies that stayed on MySpace or Foursquare for far too long. Don't make the mistake of sticking around when a channel goes from money channel to ghost channel.

Ghost Channels

Ghost channels aren't being used by your ideal audience, and they aren't being used by competition. At first glance, these channels probably seem both difficult and unnecessary to try and scale until signals start showing traction with your audience.

Gaining insight into how to use ghost channels to drive traction and results early can be an advantage, in that you could be first to tap into it as a results-driving channel. However, that comes with a risk of learning a channel that is never used by your audience. You could be learning about them, waiting in the wings, and ready to distribute when (and if) your audience enters the space.

When a ghost channel is new to the market, it is often used by an audience you may deem too young or somewhere outside a position to buy from you. However, you need to assess the channel's potential. Could you see your audience eventually being on this channel in six months, one year, or two years? Playing the long game by learning this channel early can help you tap into its potential down the road. A ghost channel today can transform into a rocket channel tomorrow. Just look at the early days of Snapchat and TikTok, where the audience was very young and did not have a lot of purchasing power. Now both channels are utilized by business-to-business brands regularly to distribute content and influence buyers.

Ghost channels can be hit or miss. I'm not saying to go all-in on every ghost channel or to invest in any single one blindly. Keep your eyes on them and assess them. Test content in them to collect metrics. These channels can go away very quickly and may never reach your ideal audience. But they nevertheless could develop and grow into an opportunity.

Questionable Channels

These channels are saturated with competition. But what's worse is that they have a low engagement rate with your target audience. They leave you scratching your head and thinking, *Why in the world are companies still leveraging this?* These channels are typically invested in long after their value has evaporated due to switching costs, outdated practices, and uninformed decision-making.

Examples might include industry magazines or random PR syndicate channels. Pushing on one of those to expand on questionable channels, industry magazines might hire a well-known individual to create content for them. The idea is that the allure of the industry magazine will boost traffic back to the guest writer's website/content while also providing the magazine with some content. Although perhaps valuable in certain niche industries, this type of content doesn't generate audiences and engagement like it used to. Print is out, for the most part. Sorry, not sorry.

Questionable channels, at one point, may have been a money or rocket channel. Competitors hang on because they were able to generate value out of it at one point. But they've been there too long. Modern consumers see through the channel's old-school, gated techniques as being disingenuous and mined of authenticity. There's a lot of production involved but very little traction.

The investment in these channels makes no sense. Every year, I see brands spending millions of dollars on print ads and brochures. Then they overflow people's mailboxes. They are paying to fill up landfills. I can remember, at my first condo, I tested the volume of my building's total discarded print-ad fliers, and I could've filled up my bedroom with the amount that came in four months. Millions of dollars spent. Millions of pieces of paper printed. All wasted.

DISTRIBUTE TO THE MOON

Out of all of the channels discussed, rocket channels offer the best chance for content traction to skyrocket. With rocket channels, brands can increase market share, which is no easy task. You want to find these channels because they're going to give you the opportunity to distribute your story effectively.

Consider how Airbnb used Craigslist as a distribution channel. They spread their listings to an audience looking for short-term rentals, and they did so without paying Craigslist a thing. Now the company is worth billions of dollars. Or, consider the impact of the greatest rocket-channel story of all time. The story of Microsoft using IBM to rocket themselves into the economic stratosphere.

In 1980, Bill Gates and Paul Allen, famous founders of Microsoft, signed a nonexclusive deal with IBM to place MS-DOS on every new IBM. The contract let Microsoft retain the right to still sell MS-DOS to other computer manufacturers. Microsoft leveraged IBM as a rocket channel because IBM, at this time, was a well-respected computer manufacturer that consumers trusted. IBM solicited software development proposals from software providers. One major sticking point for IBM was that any proposal required an NDA that prevented these developers from discussing "Project Chess," a project not of concern to this story. But, Microsoft wanted to enter this audience-heavy channel.

Many other software developers (Microsoft's competition) got caught up in the NDA and wasted time internally debating the legal mumbo-jumbo. That opened the door for Microsoft to sign the NDA and make the no-brainer choice. Signing the agreement quickly and early—or, to say it another way, by leveraging this rocket channel—Microsoft cut off their competitors who were dragging their feet. The rest is history.

Even better still, IBM *paid* Microsoft for the deal. After all, they were buying Microsoft's software. So, think of it. Microsoft received tremendous, company-and-industry-altering value from placing their product on IBM computers. And meanwhile, IBM paid them for it. It's hard to imagine that scenario today. The amount of exposure that Microsoft would receive would surely, in today's world, mean the reverse—any software company would pay IBM to tap into their audience.

In the months that followed the Microsoft-IBM deal, other PC manufacturers, especially from Japan, approached Gates about using MS-DOS. Within a year, Microsoft licensed MD-DOS to over seventy other computer manufacturers. The distribution was unprecedented. Microsoft's software became *the* PC software. To say Microsoft operating systems are the preferred choice for developers and new products is an understatement. It's almost a universal childhood experience to have drawn stick figures in Paint. Outside of Apple and Microsoft, very few computer users have heard of any other operating system brand. That's the power of distribution.

ELEMENTARY, DEAR CREATOR

You've learned the Sherlock Homeboy method. Now it's time to find, meet, and create content for your audience. Use your new skill to learn information about your target audience and to understand exactly where and how to make distribution-strategy choices based on your specific situation.

By implementing this method, you will move through the powerful sequence of channel-user fit, then content-user fit, and finally arrive at content-market fit, which is where you want to be. You'll also be able to uncover the rocket channels and money channels, which will become your best investments.

Sherlock Holmes needed the right tools. So do you. Using your brain attic, you have the opportunity to create once and distribute forever.

Now that you understand distribution basics, the next two parts in this book turn to digging deeper into each of the layers discussed, including channel-specific guides. But before channel-specific guides, you must come to know the importance of remixing and republishing. You might be thinking, *How can I distribute the same content forever?* Some say the definition of insanity is to do the same thing and expect different results. But a strong distribution strategy entails remixing and republishing old content. When it reaches the audience again, it will be fresh and new, paying never-ending dividends for you and your organization.

REMIX AND REPUBLISH

5

REMIXING CONTENT

ARKETERS COMPETE FOR ATTENTION, PLAIN AND simple.

When I was little, TV had my full attention. WWE. Gargoyles. Power Rangers. You name it, I was watching it. And my parents would always tell me not to sit too close, but I would rarely listen. They would say, "You're going to hurt your eyes," or, "Your eyes will go bad." Turns out, you can sit as close as you want to a TV, and it's kinda okay. Most of our jobs are to sit in front of a screen all day that is inches from our face. And with the rise of virtual reality, we literally are putting screens on our eyes. Why?

Because the content is that good. It's immersive. It's worth getting close to the screen for. It's worth our attention.

Once you have a piece of content that is worthy of attention, it's time to take advantage of that and get the most out of it as possible. Your goal as a creator is to capture the attention of your audience and keep it.

I'll never forget when I heard the former Netflix CEO, Reed Hastings say, "You get a show or a movie you're really dying to watch, and you end up staying up late at night, so we actually compete with sleep." This quote really speaks to the power of attention. One of the best ways to ensure you can capture attention is to stick to things that work. If you have a story, a message, or an idea or a concept that has worked on one channel in the past, it's worthwhile trying to remix it for a different channel. It's in the act of embracing the remix where some of the greatest returns can be found. Let's dive in.

WHAT IS A REMIX?

It's not just a concept in hip-hop. It's also at the heart of some of the biggest and most successful companies of all time. From Disney and Apple to Jay Z and Linkin Park— remixes have offered some of the most fascinating creations of our time.

Remixing is one of the central strategies of one of the most competitive brands in the world, The Walt Disney Company. We can debate what the real "heyday" of Disney animation was all we want. But their impressive media engine has operated on remixing content for its entire, century-long run. As a child with my face close to the TV, I watched classics like *Aladdin* (1992), *The Lion King* (1994), *Dumbo* (1941), *Mulan* (1998), and *Hercules* (1997).

These classics are based on other classics. They are remixes. *Aladdin* is based on a folk tale included in the *One Thousand and One Nights* compilation. *Dumbo* is based on a short story. *Mulan* is based on the Chinese folk tale *Ballad of Mulan*. *Hercules* is, of course, based on the hero from Greek literature.

And you might be thinking, *Gotcha, Ross!* The Lion King *is one of Disney's rare original stories.* But you'd be wrong. Certainly, there is no "Lion King" published work, per se, but it borrows the plot from Shakespeare's *Hamlet* and replaces the characters with animals. What's more, *Hamlet* itself is a remix, lifting elements of *Brutus* and *Saga of Hrolf Kraki*, among others. So, *The Lion King* is a remix of a remix. Then, *The Lion King* (1994) was remixed again for *The Lion King 2* (1998) and *The Lion King 1½* (2004). The former added elements of Shakespeare's *Romeo and Juliet*, and the latter told the 1994 film's events from an alternative point of view. In 1998, a Broadway stage adaptation of the 1994 film debuted (and won many awards). Then, Disney theme parks began (and still show) remixed staged versions, such as *Festival of the Lion King*. And, in 2019, Disney remixed it again with the new "live-action" version, *The Lion King*. I could go on, but by now I think the point has been made. The circular strategy of remixing has informed the bulk of Disney's catalog from the company's very founding. Their first work was *The Alice Comedies* (1923–1927), remixed from the famous Lewis Carroll book. And their strategy is still in play today. Pick the story, from Marvel to *Star Wars*. It's remixed material. They really are the epitome of "create once, distribute forever."

Why does Disney dominate the box office and the entertainment industry? Largely, it's because their content has stayed the same and is still valuable. The messages, stories, and characters are timeless. And it's very likely the content you've produced is timeless and high-value, especially for your target audience.

Now, I'm not saying you could become the next Disney, revenue-wise. I simply want you to key in on their winning strategy of embracing the remix.

For our purposes, remixing content means finding ways to reformat existing content across key marketing channels, tailoring that content for the various styles and expectations on each individual channel. One piece of your content can be remixed from a blog post into an e-book, then an infographic, then a video, and finally a podcast. Updating elements keeps things fresh and speaking to the latest iteration of your audience. Maybe your audience prefers vertical videos instead of limited-character tweets—where 1994's *The Lion King* utilized 2-D animation and Matthew Broderick, 2019's *The Lion King* utilized 3-D animation and Beyoncé. Same difference.

Good content remixed into the conventions of modern distribution channels will resonate with your audience. By remixing your content, you give it new life and unlock new opportunities for success. But not every organization or professional believes remixing is a worthwhile endeavor.

EMBRACE THE REMIX

Embrace the remix by looking at those who have done it well. Look to hip-hop music, which is built on the back of remixes. Hip-hop often samples other songs to create its new, modern hits. This strategy should be employed with our own content.

The opportunities that exist for content distribution are broad. You can distribute your content through paid media channels, directly to your audience, through owned channels, in niche communities, and on social media. There are hundreds of ways to distribute your content, but the remix can be the most powerful because it scales the power of each piece of content you've produced. You need to embrace the remix. Content marketing remix is the act of taking one asset and turning it into multiple, slightly adjusted assets.

If your audience is spending time on multiple channels, it's low-hanging fruit to remix your content for the channels they're spending time on. If your audience is on Twitter, remix your content into a thread. If your audience is on Instagram, remix your content for Stories. If your audience is on LinkedIn, remix your content as a LinkedIn article.

By remixing and redistributing, not only will you generate more engagement, you will also give your content a much longer, possibly infinite lifecycle. Let me demonstrate this with a personal example.

Early on in my career, I wrote a guide about how to grow engagement for Instagram marketers. It generated decent traction. Soon after, I remixed this guide into a Slideshare deck, which generated hundreds of thousands of views (and a similar amount in revenue). Eventually, I remixed it into a YouTube video, a downloadable PDF, and an online course. Then, I remixed all of these pieces of content to publish a blog about remixing, titled "Rain Drop. Drop Top.

How To Make Your Blog Never Flop, Flop." Hilarious title, right? There I outlined my remix strategy using remixed materials. Then, in 2019, I remixed the entire premise by doing the same thing, but this time with a guide for Snapchat. The first day I published my Snapchat guide, I generated tens of thousands of visits. The Slideshare version I created has generated well over a million views. And now, I'm even remixing that strategy as part of a larger distribution strategy covered in this book.

What's the moral of the story? You don't need to constantly think of the next new thing. You can translate your content into remixed versions to generate traction in the channels your audiences visit.

After creating content for a few months (or years), you can build up a reserve of valuable content. Over time, you shouldn't limit these stories to a single format or version. Instead, you should diversify them by remixing them for individual channels.

WHAT'S WORTH REMIXING?

Not all content is created equally.

Some of the content you develop is going to have a sole purpose, such as sales enablement content. But some assets will be created with the sole intent of getting the attention of hundreds of people offering you the flexibility to remix it.

The best way to validate whether or not a piece of content should be remixed is to first get that solo asset in front of as many people as possible. Once you have distributed that asset to your audience, analyze how they respond to it. If the reaction is significant—plenty of shares, leads, downloads, or whatever your value metric is—that's a sign you have content-market fit and that remixing this asset could be worthwhile.

But that doesn't mean you should expect results using this method every single time. You need to be a little humble about the remixing process. There are a lot of remixes that end up being complete flops. Disney's *The Hunchback of Notre Dame II: The Secret of the Bell* (2002) performed terribly and cost the company money. It's just one in a long line of flopped Disney remixes. Disney also flopped with *Tarzan 2: The Legend Begins* (2005), *Tron: Legacy* (2010), *Inspector Gadget 2* (2003), *Honey, We Shrunk Ourselves* (1997), *Air Bud 2: Golden Receiver* (1998), and countless more. With distribution and experimentation, failure is as abundant as success.

Don't be discouraged. Ultimately, you will be rewarded when your remixes generate far more engagement than the originals. Some will fall flat. Some will be a massive hit. And in between that oscillation is more engagement for your content and incoming revenue—not to mention, you get to collect more data about what's successful and what isn't.

So, how can you remix your content effectively? Let's look at the various ways.

Blog Post Remixes

Blog posts are one of the original formats of the internet. They are highly transferable, meaning these assets are easily remixed into other assets, and other assets can be remixed into a blog post.

What makes them a strong candidate for remixing? The written word is extremely versatile. And a long-form blog post could become a shorter blog post, which in turn could become the basis for status updates on all of your social media channels and platforms that operate in short-form text posts. You could include screenshot-thumbnail backlinks on these updates to send your subscribers or followers back to your blog post to increase traction on the original post.

The conventions of a blog post will vary depending on the space. But, generally speaking, a blog post hovers around 2,000 words, has an introduction with a careful summary, and contains four sections to divide information into separate, easily digestible takeaways for the reader.

One example might be a "How To Write a Book in 30 Days" post that has these four sections: "Structure," "Craft Story," "Productivity," and "Launch Book." Each of the four sections clearly delivers a specific value as part of a larger goal.

When it comes to blog posts, you might transformatively remix it into a different format. To transform a blog post into a new medium, you could take a portion or entire section and revise it to fit the conventional requirements of platforms like LinkedIn, Twitter, or YouTube. That would mean creating an article, a Twitter thread, or a video, respectively, from part (or all) of the content in the original post. That blog post could also be streamlined to exist as a series of slides in a presentation. From there, you could remix even more, creating an infographic that breaks out the four key points in the blog post and sending it to Pinterest or your audience's favorite social media channel for additional engagement and love. This is the way. This is the remix.

Using the blog as a reference, you could then create a thirty-minute video where you go even deeper on the same exact topic. This video could be remixed, too.

Video Remixes

Videos offer some of the most adaptable types of content for remixes, especially long-form genres like interviews, how-tos, or TED-talk-like presentations.

To remix your videos effectively, rewatch them and identify key moments based on timestamps. Then, chop up the video into short segments that provide the audience with a shorter sound bite that is engaging, quick to consume but just as impactful. These shorter clips are perfect for short-form channels such as YouTube Shorts, Instagram Reels, TikTok, Twitter, or even Facebook.

You can even extract the audio from your video. I've done this multiple times and have found some great success. I did a podcast once with a media entity called the Marketing Millennials. They had over 600k followers on LinkedIn. I took the audio from that interview and turned it into a podcast episode. It got an additional 5,000 downloads in two days.

And if it were a keynote presentation, you could use the audio from that presentation as a new podcast episode, as well.

When uploading these videos, one of the most important parts of the equation is to create a thumbnail that catches attention. At the time of writing, best practice is for the thumbnail to be the image of the person talking accompanied by the video's major takeaway or some type of text that lures the reader in. Figure 5.1 is an example of one of my YouTube thumbnails.

Here's another pro tip: If you ever appear on a podcast, ask for the raw video footage. These provide you with

Figure 5.1

plenty of remixable material. Your appearance on the podcast itself was likely a remixed delivery of content you
had already created, too. The host of the podcast probably
invited you to *podcastify*, so to speak, the ideas you created in another piece of high-traction content.

I've done around sixty podcasts, and each one has been
useful for distributing content. For one of those podcasts, I
joined the founder of *Morning Brew* to discuss how content
marketing is more like investing than most people think.
I took the raw footage from that episode and remixed it
into something great. After identifying key moments and
clipping them out, I added captions, animation, my Twitter

handle, and some graphics to really make it pop. Then I had my team distribute the content across my audience's channels. One interview ultimately became twenty different pieces of content spreading on the five or six different channels that I knew my audience was spending time on. Over time, those clips can then be reshared and embedded into future blog posts. The opportunities are endless.

Audio Remixes

It's a great format, but audio is slightly less versatile than other types. Why? Because all you're really working with is an audio clip and nothing more. Don't get me wrong, audio-only files (i.e., podcasts) do have advantages. The main advantage is that podcast networks like Spotify and Apple Podcasts are now driving millions of listeners every single month to podcast hosts, and you have an opportunity to take advantage of this reality by syndicating your audio clips to a podcast network. You don't need a two-hour podcast clip to distribute audio on Spotify. You can literally take a ten-to-thirteen-minute clip and share it as a podcast episode to reach hundreds or thousands.

You can use powerful clips—such as from commencement speeches, keynotes, and audiobooks—to connect with your audience on multiple channels. You can take elements of or an entire interview conducted to discuss your product or content and use those elements to anchor a podcast. You could also pull quotations from an audio interview or a local keynote you gave as part of a remixed blog or text-based piece of content.

Most pieces of audio content can be repurposed to video-specific channels like Instagram, Twitter, TikTok, or YouTube, as well. You just have to get creative. For example, you can create some type of audiogram—picture an animated sound wave—to visualize the file for the audience as they press play. Or, you could hire an illustrator to create a cartoon or animated experience that pairs nicely with your audio file, creating an engaging and interactive experience for the viewer.

Okay. I said audio files aren't that versatile. I kinda lied. Very quickly, one audio file can turn into dozens upon dozens of content updates.

Status Updates and Posts Remixes

Every day, brands and companies share text-based status updates to the various channels, however long or short. Some have become known for their irreverent and quirky posts, and social media has become a place where professional businesses can act a little bit more relatable. Need proof? Google "Wendy's Twitter roasts." You won't be disappointed.

For some, creating these status updates doesn't take that much time. The social media manager can spin up multiple posts a day that hit their ideal audience in a way that is engaging, educational, entertaining, and empowering. The speed at which you can sometimes create these content assets makes the barrier to entry low and the overall risk limited since the investment is so little. Because of that, it's time to consider some of these status updates as A/B tests to see if a story you're experimenting with is resonating with your audience. Updates can help you shape the voice of a brand. When you see significant engagement on a certain post or idea, you should remix it into something different.

Once, I sent a Tweet that read "Create once. Distribute forever." That Tweet got a whole bunch of retweets, and I knew I had stoked something people cared about. It caught fire, and now I'm remixing its central tenet into this long-form book you are reading now. That's right. A Tweet can become a book. Or, your status update could become a video. That video could become a carousel. And so on, and so on.

METAMORPHOSES

Just because a piece of content starts one way doesn't mean that's how it should finish. You should be confident to give your content new life. Don't hesitate to turn that blog post into a video, that video into a podcast, a pull quote from that podcast into a Tweet, and that tweet into an infographic.

The depiction of Hercules in Homer's *The Iliad*, written around 762 BCE, and Ovid's *Metamorphoses* paved the way for Disney's *Hercules* (1997). You read that correctly—Disney remixed a 2,800-year-old story, which in and of itself shows the staying power of content. Disney's decades of success has been built on the back of remixing beloved characters and stories ad nauseam. Or, I shouldn't say "ad nauseam" because, checking Disney's yearly revenue, it looks like their audience isn't getting sick of their remixing strategy anytime soon. In fact, Disney's ability to metamorphose and remix stories is the direct catalyst to it becoming the largest entertainment business in the world.

It's time for your content to undergo countless metamorphoses, too. Remix and distribute to drive better results from your content. Remixing is, without question, one of the more attractive, interesting, and effective ways to give your content more traction. And although remixing is a powerful tool in the distribution game, it's not the only way to parlay your old content into engagement and revenue. You can also publish your older content to give it new life, too. And republishing is where we'll pick up the conversation in the next chapter.

6

REPUBLISHING CONTENT

WHEN YOU WERE IN SCHOOL, DID YOU EVER wonder why your textbook had an edition number? There are, generally speaking, two reasons for textbook editions. First is that a given academic field updates ideas and needs to republish an older textbook. Second, textbooks are expensive, and updating them helps publishers maintain consistent revenue by mitigating the resale and cost-lowering effects of used textbooks. While there is some truth to both, the second reason is the primary driver of new textbook editions. (Send your complaints to your local representative.) The stakes motivating these re-publications? In the US alone, the textbook industry's market size, based on revenue, is sixteen billion dollars.[9]

The textbook industry teaches us an important lesson: there is value to be unlocked simply by republishing old content.

Surprisingly, this glowing review for republishing is not an attitude shared by many organizations. You might be triggered just by reading that idea. You've likely worked a job where you've been hammered with the same content marketing line over and over again: "Create more content!" (Or, worse yet, you may *currently* work at such a place.) Quotas will be hit if you create, create, create. It can be anxiety-inducing, in the sense that it feels like diminishing returns to constantly reinvent the wheel of content creation.

You might even get mild PTSD reflecting on your time needing to hit content creation deadlines. Obviously, creating content is one piece of the puzzle. But, as you've

---

9   "Educational Publishing and Textbook Industry Stats," *WordsRated*, November 14, 2021, https://wordsrated.com/educational-publishing-stats/.

learned on your journey through this book so far, it is only a small piece. The biggest piece is distribution, and republishing is one form of distribution often overlooked.

In the end, content doesn't need to change that much or at all. When I opened Chapter 1 with a virus analogy, there was an intention behind that. When a virus spreads, it replicates itself. Notice that as the "content" of the virus spreads across the globe for years, the content itself does not really change. It's the same, more or less. There are no virus boardrooms with virus molecules as members demanding that the virus content creators generate new viruses. There will be variants, to be sure, but the new variant will be the same old virus—the standard winter flu—that we always get.

There is an irony in attempting to create virality through a never-ending churn of new content. Replacing content with content, just like replacing one illness with another, is the opposite of virality. What is overlooked is that content stands a better chance of becoming viral if one thing is constantly being passed along. By distributing and seeding republished content in your audience's channels, you generate new website visits, content subscribers, or the metric engagements that matter to your brand. Republishing old content, rather than creating new content, is a powerful way to create the virality and growth you are looking for.

The content you published two months or two *years* ago is still valuable. Its content should be embraced and published again today. Republish your content instead of letting it collect dust. It's your diamond in the rough.

CONTENT UPDATES AND MAINTENANCE

Every year, Google announces changes in its search engine optimization algorithm. In 2022, the new algorithm aimed to place the most helpful or useful content on the first results page. This change, essentially, was Google discouraging marketers and others from manipulating their algorithm to get content on the first page.

What does that mean for you? It means scrubbing your old content, updating it, and republishing it to ensure it's valuable. If it is, it'll be findable by and useful to your audience. Pushing publish and then letting your content sit forever has now become one of the worst mistakes you can make. As your sitting content becomes more irrelevant, Google will ensure it is less visited. But there is good news. You are sitting on gold mines with your old content. And a content update could unlock that value for you.

Which content you choose to unlock and why will be covered shortly. First, I want to demonstrate the power of republishing.

One of the clearest examples of this phenomenon is Hootsuite's ability to refresh its customer acquisition content geared toward social media marketers. HootSuite's republished material created millions of dollars of value. They did it by simply republishing old content with up-to-date information and data.

Let's look specifically at Hootsuite's Instagram hashtags guide. The team originally published a blog post on the algorithm and Instagram hashtag strategies back in 2016. This asset generated less than 3,000 organic visits when it was first published. After four years, the traffic was less than 10,000. However, since the content was updated and republished in 2021, the same piece of content now generates 232,000 organic visits every month and is updated annually with new data and new dates.

What changed? Well, Hootsuite embraced content repurposing and republishing. They identified the content piece as an asset with great potential, updated it, and then republished it. Figure 6.1 shows what their republishing menu looks like for this piece.

After publishing the original content and letting it collect dust, Hootsuite updated the already existing content. Afterward, they remixed that updated content into several new formats, directing traffic back to the updated content. For example, they created a six-minute YouTube

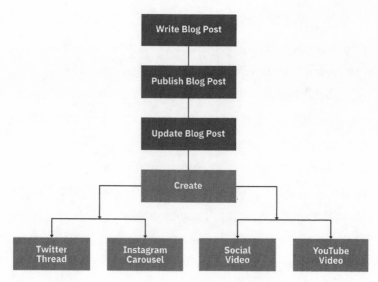

Figure 6.1

video that summarized many of the republished content's talking points.

The video performed really well, generating 21,000 views in less than a year. The brilliance I see about this specific video is that Hootsuite used long-tail keywords to break up the YouTube video into the following chapters:

- "Why use hashtags?"
- "How do hashtags work?"
- "How do you tell if your hashtag is working?"
- "How many hashtags should you use?"
- "How do you find good hashtags to use?"

- "Different categories of hashtags"
- "How do you hide your hashtags?"
- "What happens if you use a banned hashtag?"

These keywords are also featured in the long-form guide found on Hootsuite's site. At the time of writing, the question "How do hashtags work?" has 800 searches a month, and Hootsuite's guide shows up first every time to offer direction.

> How do hashtags work?   ✕ 🎤 🔍

https://blog.hootsuite.com › instagram-hashtags   ⋮ **Traf/mo** (us): 15.90K/4.59M - **Kw** (us): 788/74.4
1 Instagram Hashtags 2022: The Ultimate Guide - Hootsuite Blog
How to **use hashtags** on Instagram—7 tips and tricks — A **hashtag** is a combination of
letters, numbers, and/or emoji preceded by the # symbol (e.g., #NoFilter) ...

Figure 6.2

But Hootsuite didn't stop there. They embedded the YouTube video in the republished content and made the table of contents more robust and interesting.

Hootsuite then remixed the content to a carousel on Instagram, generating more than 1,600 reactions.

These remixes were short, digestible, and followed the conventions of each channel used. The new engagement—to the tune of several hundred thousand—came from freshening up and republishing one piece of content.

Hootsuite simply updated their 2016 hashtag guide to reflect 2021's user experience. The content they needed to update was pretty niche to a specific audience need.

In terms of how you need to freshen up content to republish it, you will be the expert on your own content and the evolving needs of your audience.

REPUBLISH REGULARLY

What type of republishing frequency is part of a successful distribution strategy? You should be republishing your content on a weekly or monthly basis. Updated and republished content is a powerful way to maintain and increase engagement while thriving. So, identify your best content and republish it on a strategic schedule for increased readership, visits, engagement, and the like. Ok sure. If we're talking about a website that has just a few blog posts, you might not need to republish weekly or monthly. But if you're well established and have the resources to do it, the ROI can be significant.

Before you think republishing isn't worth your time, think about the world's most famous book: the Bible. The Bible continues to be published in many different languages and formats. Versions with modern text, modern language, and more. Some of the most influential texts of our times flourish precisely because they are republished.

Things do change. Technologies change. Social norms change. But many things stay constant. Humans still operate under the same range of emotions they always have. The chemicals that make up our universe are constant and unchanging. Stories and content can stay relevant forever, and it's in your best interests to apply modern principles to those timeless pieces of content, so your return on investment for them scales.

REPUBLISHING AS AN INVESTMENT

Think like an investor who acquires stocks and bonds. Investors expect to produce dividends in the future from stocks. Content is such an investment. Hold onto its value. When the time is right, extract that value through republishing. In this way, you can optimize your content for years, like an investment that pays continuous dividends.

That begs the question: How can you identify old content that might benefit the most from a refresh and republish? A good place to start is with your greatest hits. To understand them, be able to have or acquire answers to the following questions:

- What content has generated the most traffic for you?
- What content generates the most backlinks for you?
- What content generates the most sales for you?

Further, use analytics (such as Google Analytics) as well as customer relationship management software to determine which of your assets to invest in to maximize your return on said investments.

You can also improve the value of your mediocre content or the proverbial equities you once thought were a downside investment. To republish your content, you will need to review it, make updates, and launch it again as if it's brand new. That means you have the opportunity to make previously mediocre content excellent, especially if there is some kernel of an idea that may resonate with your audience. How do you do that successfully? You identify pieces of content that might not have been developed in full. Then, continue to develop that kernel using content update strategies, such as adding new and valuable sections, including new research and data that reflects on the topic, offering third-party quotes, and so on. Apply all of the updating strategies in a rigorous and complete manner.

In some cases, content won't need to be updated or refreshed at all. You simply need to republish it. Why? Because people who follow you today aren't always the exact same people who followed you six months ago when you published that content the first time.

ACTIONABLE CONTENT UPDATE STRATEGIES

With the education out of the way, let's look at some actionable steps that you can implement when republishing your content. Even though your work will be unique to you, the following are some basic, universal elements of maintenance to include in all content updates.

- **Dates**: People want relevant, recent content with current trends and stories.

- **New Research and Data**: Any information or data you reference must be up-to-date and accurate. Research needs to be as relevant and timely as possible to resonate with your audience. Not only will that give you credibility with your users, it will also help you when they search for your keywords. Google knows if you're linking to old content.

- **Story Adjustment**: The stories and anecdotes in content may need to be updated with the times, because changes in social norms or a topical anecdote have aged out of your audience's experience. Make sure your content is relevant to today and your audience.

- **New Takeaways**: Are there new things for people to understand about the topic? Add original takeaways, strategies, or techniques worth noting. If you do so, the audience will feel the updated content is both relevant and well-rounded.

- **Third-Party Quotes**: Think about adding a quotation from an industry expert or well-known influencer in your space. That can ground the content in a sense of authority that speaks to your audience's needs (and make the search engine algorithm happy). A quotation could also come from a specialized expert on your team. Consider soliciting a quotation from a third party by reaching out via email or other channels.

- **Embed Video Content and Podcasts**: This is a republishing strategy but also a search engine optimization strategy. As YouTube's parent company, Google loves YouTube. Currently, when you embed videos in old content, Google's algorithm is more willing to send traffic your way. As traffic flows to that YouTube video, your growing subscribers can increase content engagement on your other platforms.

- **Offer Downloadable Templates**: Utility is at the heart of B2B marketing. If you can arm people with free tools, templates, checklists, and resources, they will thank you for making their lives easier. Updating content should help your audience as much as it helps you. To receive value, you need to give value.

- **Add New and Valuable Sections**: Go above and beyond by creating new sections in your blog that are highly actionable and insightful. Swap fluff for practicality.

- **Improve the Visuals**: Design tastes change. Make sure you're creating and using visuals that are aligned with today's internet aesthetics. Keep things fresh.

When looking at the big picture of all the above strategies, mix and match them, but make sure you implement many of them for any given piece of content, not just one.

When you review your content, it should hopefully be clear to you which strategies would be most beneficial. Updating your content strategically means you are treating your content like a long-term investment.

TIME TO TRANSFORM YOUR PERSPECTIVE

While gurus may tell you that new content is where the money lies, they are lying. You should identify the existing content in your library that drives value and update it. Republish old pieces with new information on a regular basis, as that could drive potentially millions of dollars worth of traffic in your lifetime. So, it is worth it.

Here's a hot take: If you're reading this and it's later in the year than March, some of you probably don't need to produce any more content this year. I know that might sound wild, but your content portfolio has probably enough assets to help you remix and republish your way into new revenue streams. Create once, distribute forever.

But republishing and remixing isn't the only part of a successful distribution strategy. And since I promised that this guide would be tactical, it's time to turn your attention to a breakdown of how to distribute on each distribution channel. Let's get tactical.

III
CHANNEL-
BY-CHANNEL
GUIDE

STOP: This is important. The upcoming chapters are a channel-by-channel guide for distribution. Depending on your unique situation, it is highly unlikely that your content or product will thrive by distributing your content on all of them. In fact, I wouldn't encourage you to do that. In the same way that no chef is great at cooking BBQ, Mexican, Sushi, Italian, Creole, *and* African Cuisine, it's rare that you find a brand that thrives in every channel. Find the channel that aligns best with your industry and study the recommendations in this book.

The intent for this portion of the book is not necessarily to read it from start to finish. Consider it a "choose your own adventure" guide. I want you to feel encouraged to read only the chapters or strategies that are relevant to your situation. If, later on down the line, your audience shifts and is present in a channel you didn't read about in your first go around, you can always come back and consume what you need when you need.

Here is a list of Part 3's chapters to help guide your reading.

- Chapter 7: Email Distribution
  - Strategy 1: Existing Mailing List
  - Strategy 2: Third-Party Email Lists
  - Strategy 3: One-to-One Email Outreach
  - Strategy 4: Existing Email Funnels
  - Strategy 5: Outbound Sales Distribution

- Chapter 8: Social Media Distribution
  - LinkedIn Strategies
  - X (Formerly Twitter) Strategies
  - Facebook Strategies
  - Instagram Strategies
  - TikTok Strategies

- Chapter 9: Partnership Distribution
  - Strategy 1: Joint Webinar Partnership
  - Strategy 2: Distribution through Aggregators
  - Strategy 3: Guest Blog Posts
  - Strategy 4: Product and Platform Distribution
  - Strategy 5: Newsletter Partnerships

- Chapter 10: Community Distribution
  - Facebook Group Strategies
  - Subreddit Strategies
  - Slack Strategies
  - Discord Strategies

- Chapter 11: Search Distribution
  - SEO Distribution Strategies
  - Paid Search Distribution Strategies

EMItimes
DISTRIBUTION

'VE MANAGED HUNDREDS OF EMAIL LISTS. WHETHER
it's email lists for clients or my own brands, I've seen it all.
In that time, email has become one of my favorite channels to use for distribution.

I always say that email is undefeated because, while
every other channel changes its algorithm, email stays
pretty much the same. I'm also obsessed with the immedi-
acy of ROI. One email can drive millions in revenue within
a matter of hours. And as you build your own skills on this

channel, you will start to see that the ROI is not just in revenue but also in the relationships.

But before I go any further, the stakes need to be discussed. Email marketing campaigns will send out messages to hundreds, thousands, tens of thousands, or hundreds of thousands of people. It can be surprising that, number one, you will get folks who are excited, ecstatic, or thrilled to have heard about the opportunity, new idea, or story that you have created and shared. Number two, it could very well be that one of these excited people becomes a new lead and revenue generator for you.

For example, I started a newsletter in 2014. Since then, many of my subscribers have worked at the largest companies in the world, such as Stripe, Salesforce, Nike, and the like. If there's a company with marketers striving to get better at growth and distribution, I've likely engaged with that company at some point through my newsletter and email list.

And when I send an email to my newsletter subscribers, I'll receive "thank you" and "this made my day" messages, which are all nice and appreciated. But what's even more appreciated is when the response has the intention of doing business with me. That's what happened when my email about Instagram marketing led to an engagement from the CEO of a major beverage company. He was holding a conference in Orlando, Florida. In hopes I would speak at the conference, he offered me (as part of my speaking contract) an all-expenses-paid trip to Walt Disney World and Resorts for my family and a nice check. Win-win.

These win-win opportunities are possible when you leverage email distribution. It's my hope that you are able to leverage email distribution yourself, spreading your content to the right audience to help your brand grow.

THE VALUE OF EMAIL

If you can build up your email list, it can be a powerful distribution tool.

A person's email is the most valuable information you can capture. Why? People will maintain their email for way longer than their social media profiles or handles. Typically, an individual will hold the same email that they had right out of university for the rest of their life.

Having access to your audience for possibly the rest of their life is a valuable asset. Over the course of that time, one email hitting the right eyes at the right time can turn into transformative opportunities for revenue. And in this chapter, I will talk about some of the different ways in which email as a distribution channel can be leveraged.

EMAIL DISTRIBUTION STRATEGIES

Email distribution is the act of distributing your story, content, or product to your ideal customer and audience via an email exchange. The word "exchange" is important in that last sentence, because even though an email list sends a mass message to everybody on the list, it often needs to be engineered in such a way that makes each email feel like a personal letter exchanged between two people.

For that reason, the second important information to capture (after their actual email) is the subscriber's first and last name. This will help you personalize those emails so you can speak directly to those individuals. Potential customers who feel consistently connected to a brand are more apt to reciprocate. It reminds me of what Dale Carnegie said: "Remember that a person's name is, to that person, the sweetest and most important sound in any language." By emphasizing the subscriber's, they feel seen and realized.

When using an email list, there are a variety of strategies to consider. For the rest of this chapter, and with the basic definitions and tactics out of the way, let's look at various email list strategies and how you might implement them for distribution optimization. For each strategy, I'll start by listing its major goal and my assessment of its difficulty. The purpose of each is to give you the ability to instantly assess if the strategy is right for you or if you may want to move on to the next strategy in this chapter.

Disclaimer: Throughout this chapter and the rest of Part 3, I start each strategy with a brief "Goal" and "Difficulty Rating." Because Part 3 is a choose-your-own adventure, use these quick descriptors to discern whether or not the strategy is right for you.

Additionally, the system I will implement for the Difficulty Rating is a scale from zero to ten, with ten being "extremely difficult" and zero being "extremely easy." The intention is to give you clarity about what you face.

Strategy 1: Existing Mailing List

- **Goal**: Drive referral traffic from emails.
- **Difficulty Rating**: 8/10

One of the key ways to leverage an existing mailing list is to do the work to build up that mailing list. Ideally, you have an existing mailing list of former, current, and potential clients (or subscribers). If not, set up a landing page where you can capture first name, last name, and the email of visitors to your website. No matter if you are a small coffee shop collecting business cards for a free latte or a sophisticated SaaS company that happens to run paid media campaigns to generate leads, those leads make up the mailing list and create a way to drive traffic and generate revenue.

GROWING YOUR MAILING LIST

You can also build your list by letting people know that you have a mailing list you use to provide value at its publishing interval. An example Twitter post might read: "Did you know every Tuesday I send an email about systems analytics? Subscribe at the link below and join the 12,000 others who get this insight weekly."

Call to actions (CTAs) on your website also works to build a mailing list. It could be a banner at the top of your website, or you could have CTAs throughout your site in the form of text, display ads, or pop-ups. You can offer free or discounted assets to your potential customers, asking for their email in exchange. You can use these methods daily. If your content and distribution are strong, you should have a plethora of people signing up.

As you build your list, it's quality over quantity. The size of your mailing list matters, to be sure. What matters more, though, is the quality of the people who make up your mailing list. If you have a mailing list of 50,000 people, but your analytics show nobody is opening the email or clicking on links, then that's not a high-value list. The whole point of sending an email is to create something of value and give it to people who want that value. They should be clicking on your email content, consuming it, learning from it, and fired up to learn more. I would rather have a 500-person mailing list where 400 of those people are my exact audience and are opening every single email.

DRIVE TRAFFIC FROM YOUR MAILING LIST

With a mailing list in hand, your goal is to drive referral traffic from this existing list of relevant people directly to your content and website. People subscribe to your newsletter or mailing list because they care about your ideas, want to learn from you, or are interested in hearing more about things you share. This means you should strive to always incorporate recent, relevant, and valuable content in your emails to validate the subscriber's decision to give you their email address. Confirm that they made the right decision and create a newsletter that is worth telling the world about, making it clear to others how much value you deliver to inboxes regularly.

As you publish new blog posts, launch podcasts, remix old stories, or republish content, understand that the links to these pieces should be distributed to your mailing list to drive traffic. Let your subscribers know when a new piece of content has gone live on your website by sending an email and you might be surprised how powerful this channel can be.

One way to be even more sophisticated with your email distribution efforts is to ask subscribers what type of content they are interested in. You can do this indirectly by placing a link or button to a survey near the email signature to solicit feedback or the topics of future emails. Just like with using first name and last name, soliciting participation from the customer creates a connected, personalized feeling. So, their feedback is extremely valuable to you and can actually result in better email segmentation. For example, if people select that they want "beginner content," you can create a list for beginners and a list for "experts," sending each group content tailored to their needs.

The difficulty of leveraging your existing mailing list is an eight out of ten. Building a mailing list is not easy. People are very afraid to give up their email because of the amount of spam companies pound into their inboxes every day. It's a difficult bias to overcome. But once you capture an email, it allows you to distribute your content to someone for a very long time.

To overcome the hurdle of fear of spam, you need to show the potential subscriber that you will be responsible with their email. Do this by calling it out on the landing page. Do this by only emailing them information of value. And be clear you won't be spamming them with a plethora of emails. This is how you earn your customer's trust.

Strategy 2: Third-Party Email Lists

- **Goal**: Get users of other people's channels to subscribe to your newsletter.
- **Difficulty Rating**: 9/10

I like to call third-party email lists "OPCs"—other people's channels. They are an opportunity to share your content through the use of somebody else's well-established email list. I think OPCs are one of the most powerful forces on the internet and a true cheat code to driving new levels of growth. OPCs give you access to an already-made audience that may or may not have familiarity with your brand. Further, distribution through OPCs is a powerful way to scale your content's reach. Using these third-party email lists to distribute your content can provide major benefits to creators and brands who use this channel to spread high-value content.

Pro Tip: Leveraging a third-party list is all about collaboration. It's kind of like when a musician from one genre crosses over with a musician from another genre to create a smash hit. If you've added value to your fan base for years and they love you, then you collaborate with another brand or creator to have your content distributed in their newsletter. With that, you now have the opportunity to win new fans and get new followers. That's the power of OPCs. So always aim to bring your best content to these. It's key to winning fans who will subscribe, buy, follow, and work with you for years to come.

FINDING THE RIGHT THIRD-PARTY LIST

It all starts with finding a brand or individual with an email list you actually want to see turn into your own audience. When looking to leverage third-party email lists, seek alignment between your audience and the other newsletter's audience. For example, it wouldn't make sense for me to share my marketing content in a newsletter focused on plant-based food. Not only would I drive very little or no traffic to my marketing website, but I probably cost the owner of that newsletter a lot of their own subscribers.

How do you find alignment? Google is your best friend. If you are a vegan content creator that needs a vegan food newsletter, type in things like "plant-based newsletters" or "vegan newsletters," and in doing so you will be met with a handful of newsletters that are serving this demographic. Simply use the keywords that describe your industry and the word newsletter, and you will find a ton of opportunities for collaboration.

After you find the third-party mail lists, what do you do? You reach out to the owner of the list directly and let them know that you have created content that you believe their audience will find value in. Find their email online. Many people list their contact information on their website. Check their LinkedIn. Send them a DM on Twitter. If the owner is savvy, they will understand that your content will save them from needing to cobble together something for their newsletter this week and see this as a win.

Here is a quick template of a reach-out email to deliver to a newsletter owner.

Hey, [first name]

I love what you are doing with your newsletter, [insert newsletter name here]. Its content is inspiring, as is your commitment to add value to the lives of your audience week after week.

Like you, I strive to deliver value to those who need it. I just wrote a piece titled [insert title of your content here] that I think your audience will find valuable.

You don't have to reply to this. You don't even have to use this. But feel free to share this piece with your audience if you think it's valuable.

Either way, I'm rooting for you, sharing for you, and I love what you're doing for the community.

All the best,

[Insert your name and email signature.]

You'll notice that this email is not asking directly to share the piece in the newsletter. It's low-pressure, praises the owner's work authentically, and leaves the ball in their court. The email clearly demonstrates I know their material, subscribe to their material, and hope for their continued success. People are more likely to reciprocate and respond positively the more they feel connected to the person, so the email has inserted that authentic connection. Feel free to remix this template and use it.

SPONSORING A THIRD-PARTY LIST

If you have a budget, consider sponsoring a third-party newsletter. Essentially, you would make a deal where you compensate the newsletter owner a certain amount of money in exchange for your content showing up in their newsletter. This is something my company, Foundation Marketing, has been doing for quite some time. Major brands want access to our audience, and they pay us on a regular basis to show up in our bi-weekly newsletter. Why? Because it makes sense for them to reach marketers directly rather than through roundabout channels. Sponsoring our newsletter gives them precise industry exposure.

The difficulty of leveraging third-party email lists is a nine out of ten—unless, of course, you're paying for the reach. If you're paying for the reach it's a two out of ten. Everyone likes money. So it becomes easy. But most people who have a newsletter of their own do not want to amplify other people's content unless it's really, really good. Most third-party list owners want to send traffic to their own websites. It's understandable. That's why ensuring alignment between your audience and theirs is such a key selling point to get them to share your content. Or, you can offer an exchange. You could share some of their content with your mailing list for them after they've done so for you. I've done this with newsletters like MorningBrew,

Trapital, and more. The results have always been a major spike in our subscribers and the other list.

This distribution strategy is also difficult because some spaces are fairly niche and small. Reaching out to niche third parties might not be possible because, quite simply, there may be no third party with content and audience alignment. In that case, you're in luck. You might want to create a mailing list that redefines your industry.

Strategy 3: One-to-One Email Outreach

- **Goal**: Capture the attention of a highly relevant individual to your work.
- **Difficulty Rating**: 9/10

If you are looking for a specific individual to see your story—a highly relevant individual or target customer—one-to-one email outreach can be an amazing way for you to unlock revenue opportunities. "Highly relevant individual" means ideal customers, dream clients, industry leaders, CEOs, and people with massive audiences. They are people who can further distribute your content on your behalf.

RESEARCH YOUR AUDIENCE

One-to-one email outreach is difficult to scale, but it can be one of the most powerful ways to get your content distributed. The goal is to capture the attention of an ideal customer to your business. How do you do that? Research, research, research. Start by understanding exactly who it is you're looking to connect with. You want to understand their motivations, their business, their goals, their situation, and their audience. Understand their purpose. Understand why you want them and their audience to consume your content. Peruse their LinkedIn, Twitter, and other social media platforms to get a better understanding of who they are and their interests. It can help you tailor your content for them. Make it obvious that you did your research.

If necessary, uncover their email using email research tools. There are tools that exist, including Hunter and Anymail Finder, to help you find the emails of the people you want to connect with.

CONSTRUCTING A BESPOKE EMAIL

Be friendly, nonaggressive, and personalized. Similarly to third-party email list owners, don't directly ask them to look at or share your content. Frame the email in such a manner that they understand you're making them aware you've published something they or their team may find valuable.

Consider how this template demonstrates nonaggression and highly personalized messaging.

Hey, [target's first name]

It's so cool to see a fellow Husky in the world of marketing. I graduated two years before you. If you were anywhere near Elm Hall, it's very possible we crossed paths at some point. Feels like forever ago. But that's not why I'm reaching out today.

I'm reaching out to let you know I just pressed publish on an article that breaks down [insert their pain point or aligned audience's pain point] that I think you and your team will really enjoy.

I interviewed X number of founders to put this piece together, and I think it's something that you will love. If you or your team have any questions about this piece, by all means, feel free to reach out. I know your company just [insert milestone here] and would love to talk about this further if it's of interest, but no pressure.

I'll follow up in a couple of weeks to see if you have any other questions. Have a great day. Go Huskies!

[Insert your name and email signature.]

Once you've sent this targeted individual an email, you don't want to be the person who is following up every two hours. Instead, follow up one more time at exactly the time you indicated in your original email. Keep the email short and sweet, and ask if they have any questions. Something simple will do the trick. These people are busy.

The difficulty for email outreach is nine out of ten. Because you have to generate this outreach on a one-to-one basis, it has to be highly personalized. That means a few things. First, you need to fully understand the psychographics of this person in order to maximize effectiveness and empathy. Don't forget: they didn't opt-in to receive this email, so they will be on the defensive when they see it. Second, you (or someone on your team) will have to thoughtfully compose the email. Both the research and the writing mean this is difficult and takes time. One-to-one email outreach can be intimidating and difficult, but it can ultimately unlock a wave of new opportunities.

Strategy 4: Existing Email Funnels

- **Goal**: Reengage people inside your existing email funnels with content.
- **Difficulty Rating**: 3/10

What is an email funnel? Essentially, it's a strategic and precise series of emails designed to nurture subscribers to turn them into visitors, customers, and raving fans. The funnel starts when someone takes an activity like downloading a resource and then is met with a series of emails strategically planned and scheduled to build rapport. This strategy is usually accomplished successfully by using a user's information to send emails that are more likely to resonate with their needs and lead to a sale.

Email funnels are run when an audience is in place and aware of your brand overall. Many organizations, for example, will offer free downloads, case studies, webinars, cheat sheets, events, and master classes. To get access to this content, an organization might ask to capture basic information, such as first name, last name, and email address. Afterward, they move these subscribers through their funnel until a business outcome occurs.

CREATING AN EMAIL FUNNEL

How can you create an email funnel? Identify a few key areas on your website or within your product where your visitors find the most value. That could be requesting a demo, signing up for a newsletter, downloading a template, or any number of already mentioned value touchpoints that result in them giving you their email.

You don't want the user to give you their information and the relationship be done. This shouldn't be their last touchpoint with your content. When you capture their email through a funnel, you begin to nurture that relationship with a series of emails that add additional value and sell your offering.

Most email marketing software provides highly tailored and personalized functionality where you can use their first name directly in the email, making it personalized to them or their company name (if you have that data available). This makes the emails feel even more human. To take it a step further, if you know what content a specific subscriber is clicking on, your follow-up emails can be automatically set up to point them back to other, already-made content on your website that aligns with the content they clicked earlier. Here is an example of what a funnel system could look like:

- **Day one**: User downloads a PDF.
- **Day one, two hours later**: User receives an email with a link to the PDF for future use.
- **Day three**: User receives an email asking if they enjoyed the value of the PDF with a link to a highly converting article.
- **Day six**: User receives an email sharing a new-to-the-user piece of content that was published four months ago but highly valuable based on their website activity.

- **Day ten**: User receives a high-value case study that showcases how they can leverage your product or solution.
- **Day fourteen**: User receives an email with content that all newsletter subscribers have indicated is extremely valuable and crucial to their success.
- **Day sixteen**: User receives a final email that sends one more highly valuable asset for free. Included in this email is an explanation that the user will now be subscribed to the newsletter and that, if they have any questions about services, they should feel free to reach out.

By creating a funnel that's constantly distributing your already-made content, it will be continuously redistributed in the inboxes of hundreds of people every week. This is free traffic; you set this funnel once and forget it.

The difficulty level for existing email funnels is three out of ten. Essentially, you set a funnel up once, and after the setup cost is offset by the initial incoming revenue, it's all profits and results after that. I have funnels that are six years old that still pay at least two car payments for me a year. You can update it as needed, but you are giving yourself the mechanism that grows your reach.

Strategy 5: Outbound Sales Distribution

- **Goal**: Drive direct traffic from the sales team to the assets you've produced.
- **Difficulty Rating**: 5/10

At a certain scale, if you have a sales team, you have an awesome distribution opportunity. Yes, your sales team presents an opportunity to drive sales, but they also have an opportunity to distribute your content. Every single day, your sales team is talking to exactly the right audience about their pain points and problems. Most sales teams send hundreds of emails each week, and each of those emails presents an opportunity for your content to spread.

The sales team is an often-overlooked distribution asset, especially in the B2B space where folks tend to view sales as driving direct revenue rather than a marketing apparatus. But the truth is this: If you can inspire your sales team to embrace distribution, it can give you amazing reach. With a sales team as a distribution channel, your goal is to drive direct traffic from your sales team to the assets your content team has produced.

CREATING OUTBOUND SALES DISTRIBUTION

How do you create outbound sales distribution? It starts by hosting educational sessions to ensure complete alignment across functions. Most marketing and sales teams are siloed and rarely talk to one another. If you can get over that hurdle by educating the sales team on your strategy, you will be more likely to get them to buy into the distribution efforts. Every great leader and marketer needs to take accountability for the education and training of your team. Teach your sales team the role marketing plays in moving a prospective lead through the buyer's journey and how they can play a role. If you can, then teach your sales team how outbound sales benefits from distribution by adding more pipeline to the engine—it becomes a win for everybody.

Keeping on the education train, consider sharing content with your sales team to help them learn on their own time. That could mean sending them links to content, via your internal communication channels like Slack or Teams, or recording videos talking through the process. The bottom line is you are trying to shape the culture internally so people understand and embrace the importance of content distribution. If everyone in the organization wants the same outcome, teaching them that distribution facilitates outcomes can be a powerful leadership moment that drives revenue.

Empowering your outbound sales team to be a part of your distribution engine earns a difficulty rating of five out of ten. It can be moderately challenging to convince the sales team that content distribution is worthwhile because they're already busy. Often, salespeople only care about their individual sales quota. They don't have the organization's brand and marketing at the forefront of their mind. Many of them don't care to send clients blog posts or freely downloadable PDFs...until it helps them close deals. It becomes your job, then, to educate your sales team on the value added that content marketing brings to the table to increase their close rate.

But keep in mind it all starts at the top. You need to have buy-in from the leadership on both sides of sales and marketing to increase the likelihood of this distribution channel being a successful one. Leadership must be in sync to roll out an outbound sales distribution strategy via email. Get alignment between these groups and then educate the sales team. It could inspire your sales team to distribute content forever.

THE EMAIL ADVANTAGE

There are many reasons email distribution offers value for your content, product, or organization. The two primary benefits are distribution longevity and capturing an audience that is tailored to your ideal customer.

When it comes to longevity, email is powerful because email addresses rarely change. More than any other channel you'll ever use, email will keep you connected to your audience for the most extensive amount of time. That in and of itself makes it an incredibly valuable channel, if not the most valuable. When you build an email list that aligns with your ideal customer, it becomes even more valuable.

And that brings us to capturing your ideal audience. An email distribution strategy only works if your audience wants to consume your content. You can have the largest email distribution channel in the world, but if your subscribers aren't engaging with your emails, then it may as well be worthless. Instead, cultivate an audience that deeply cares about what you have to offer in order to make your email strategies sing.

Here's a reality that I wish more people understood: You are always one email away from living a completely different life. When I was a kid, I wanted to travel the world and, because of my email distribution strategy, I have been able to see parts of the world I'd never dreamed of seeing. Beyond traveling, I also always wanted to run a multimillion-dollar business. Guess what? Email distribution helped me achieve that goal, too. Every week, I send an email to our mailing list. Someone at one of the most successful brands in SaaS in the world replies by asking to hop on a call to discuss how we can work together, and history is made. This strategy can help you achieve your goals as well. Emails can get you into the room with amazing people who can fundamentally alter the trajectory of your business. So don't sleep on the power of email distribution.

Email is one of the most valuable channels in the world, but we can't sleep on the others. Among them, social media is one of the fastest-growing opportunities in the world of distribution. Because of its expanding influence and ability to, one day soon, compete with email, I'll tackle it in the upcoming chapter.

8

SOCIAL MEDIA DISTRIBUTION

UP. UP. DOWN. DOWN. LEFT. RIGHT. LEFT. RIGHT. B. A. Start.

Cheat codes aren't just for video games. They can be harnessed for social media distribution, too.

How did I make that discovery? As a young kid, shows like *Mad Men* and movies like *Boomerang* (shout out to Marcus Graham) inspired me to get into advertising. As mentioned, my biggest obstacle was my location. When I first graduated university in rural Nova Scotia, I knew that I needed to reach people who were in my ideal agencies and industries. So I created lists of the folks I was targeting and sought them out on LinkedIn, Twitter, Facebook, and other social media platforms. I engaged with them on a regular basis with the hopes of making connections and breaking into the circles they had already established.

Like a cheat code, social media allowed me to shorten the long reach of my physical location. At that time in Nova Scotia, in my parents' basement, I had amassed maybe around 2,000 followers across all of my social media channels and networks. Pretty good, I thought. After unlocking some of the circles I actively sought, my followers across multiple channels increased to upwards of 120,000. Increasing my followers by 5,900 percent using one strategy, I'd argue, is a cheat code of distribution.

The power of social media, and the strategies to spread your reach on their platforms, first require building up followers so that you can say with confidence that, every time you push publish, thousands of people will be there ready to consume your content. You can go from being a nobody in the middle of Nova Scotia to having a massive network for successful content distribution.

BASICS OF SOCIAL MEDIA DISTRIBUTION

Before I define social media distribution, I want to reiterate the approach to this part of the book. Although every single idea discussed here can accelerate your social media success, the information might not serve everyone. If you already know which channels resonate with your audience, feel free to choose your own adventure; go directly to the channel that is most relevant to you.

Now, the definition. Social media distribution is the act of actually taking your assets and spreading them on the various social media channels in which your audience is spending time. That may sound simple, but there are a ton of new and legacy social media channels in existence. There are, in fact, hundreds of social media platforms. In 2022, six of those channels claim to have over a *billion* users. As you are reading these words, another social media channel has popped up. And another one. Oh, there's another one. Stop reading and start posting to stay caught up! (Just kidding.)

It's okay that there are so many channels. Don't feel overwhelmed. Instead, realize an opportunity exists to uncover which channels your audience spends their time. When you identify them, it becomes a process of learning the best practices and then distributing your tailored content.

In this chapter, we will dive into some of the most used channels and how to leverage them for your own purposes. However, I need to insert a disclaimer. The biggest risks you will face are twofold:

1. Being subjected to a channel's algorithm, which can turn on a dime, and
2. Fluctuations on what's trending.

For example, an algorithm could be skewed heavily towards video content one day and shift to text posts the next. These are things that you have to be aware of, meaning that, at times, you will have to reach beyond this book to figure out the current state of a channel. You want to invest in channels you think could stand the test of time, because some might disappear very quickly. Use your own marketing or business skills to forecast your expectations with each channel to decide what's best for your content or product.

That sounds like a lot of homework, but it's probably the most valuable homework you could give yourself. Why? Social media is the most prolific distribution channel we have currently. It's ubiquitous, in terms of the attention it captures from people's daily likes. It's there when people wake up and right before they fall asleep. Before they kiss their spouse good morning, people reach for their phone and check their social media.

Without any further ado, let's dive into channel-specific analysis and strategy.

LINKEDIN STRATEGIES

- **Goal**: Drive referral traffic to your content assets on your website or product. Secondarily, distribute your content natively on LinkedIn to drive engagement on this platform.
- **Difficulty Rating**: 7/10

LinkedIn is *the* professional network. The vast majority of people who use LinkedIn are talking about business, learning about their colleagues or peers, and clicking on or sharing professional content. There is no question that LinkedIn maintains its leadership position as an authority network for the professional world.

Users have the opportunity to share many different types of assets. Because of that variety, organizations on LinkedIn can connect with audiences on a mass scale, a one-to-one scale, and everything in between.

Your primary goal with this channel is to drive referral traffic from LinkedIn to assets that live on your website.

A secondary goal is to increase your following to build a long-term relationship with people on a more one-to-one basis. A further benefit: the more engagement you have, the more you open yourself up to networking opportunities and build awareness for your brand.

The first thing you need to know when sharing content on LinkedIn is the type of content that you should share there. A framework I love to rely on is what Katt Stearns and I call the "Four *E*'s of Content." And, spoiler alert, you'll be hearing about these four principles quite a bit from here on out. With each new channel and chapter, I will explain how to implement the Four *E*'s for channel-specific content.

The Four E's

The Four *E*'s are engaging, educational, entertaining, and empowering. Anything you share on LinkedIn needs to do two things:

1. Reflect each of those four elements, and
2. Do so in a manner specific to the conventions of LinkedIn.

As I discuss each concept, I will offer LinkedIn-specific implementation strategies.

ENGAGING

Engaging content inspires dialogue. It gets people talking. Hopefully that conversation happens directly on the piece of content in the form of comments. When users tag their colleagues and bring that referral traffic to your content, you get free amplification and promotion of your work.

Here's a pro tip. Engaging content on LinkedIn—and everywhere really—is often spurred by a question. People want to answer questions. And LinkedIn users are more likely to post in the form of answering questions rather than creating native content.

EDUCATIONAL

Educational content simply provides people with information framed as a teaching tool. The presumption is that the user is visiting this content, in part, to learn something new.

For LinkedIn, the educational content users desire is, as you might have guessed, professional in nature. It could teach them certain things about their role. It could present new research, statistical analysis, or information related to a specific industry. You could even post updates educating your audience about some new aspect of your product.

Educational content you curate can establish your credibility and authority within an industry, especially if your content is consumed and amplified by other folks with established authority.

ENTERTAINING

Entertaining content puts a smile on the user's face or makes them feel some sort of positive emotion, like inspiration. Content can use entertaining elements as the primary narrative driver, subtly in the content's background, or anywhere in between. How much entertainment you inject into your content depends on the channel you use.

Entertaining content does extremely well on LinkedIn. However, you don't necessarily want to go all-in on entertaining and leave out the other elements discussed. Users typically expect LinkedIn's content to be boring and professional. Entertainment is outside of the norm but a pleasant surprise. If you can break your user out of the humdrum atmosphere of LinkedIn with a pick-me-up piece of entertaining content, you are likely to generate a lot of engagement, comments, and shares. Just don't overdo it.

Even better, LinkedIn recently added a "funny" reaction. Because of the aforementioned seriousness usually associated with the channel, this reaction is an opportunity to send your content to the moon. If your content is able to generate a lot of "funny" reactions, that's a great signal you're going in the right direction, entertainment-wise.

EMPOWERING

This content celebrates someone or something other than yourself. If you're a brand, it might celebrate people on your team or even your customers. Or, if you want to take this a step further, this content might celebrate inspirational or innovative people who are in your industry.

For LinkedIn purposes, empower people who are up-and-comers in your industry and who have overcome obstacles unique to their background and identity. Everybody loves a good success story. By empowering professionals, it's going to release a lot of endorphins for the consumers of your post. It will make them feel inspired, happy you helped them stumble upon something worth celebrating, and likely ready to come back to your content for more inspiration.

Generating a connection between your brand and inspiration is a very powerful way to unlock the potential of LinkedIn.

LinkedIn's Social Rules

Beyond the Four *E*'s, the next step is to understand the social rules of LinkedIn. As mentioned, it's a professional network. Users should strive to keep things somewhat professional. Is it okay to share things about your family? Of course. Is it okay to share that you go to the gym or enjoy a glass of wine? Definitely. I am not telling you to not share that content. Just make sure to lead with professionalism.

Further, my advice would be to avoid religion, politics, or hot-button ideologies on LinkedIn. On the one hand, it may seem advantageous to post about these topics, as they will likely generate a lot of traction in the form of comments. However, these things could alienate your audience or even get you banned. Be careful about content that provokes.

Content Formats and Best Practices

With the subject matter clarified, what about the medium of LinkedIn content? This channel allows text posts, video posts, graphics, and so much more. It's important when you distribute your content to understand the range of possibilities LinkedIn offers. Embrace the idea of getting creative within LinkedIn's limitations.

Let's say you have created new content on your website, and your ultimate goal is to provide LinkedIn users a link to send them to that content. You could record a simple video of you in your office talking about the new piece of content, highlighting the major takeaways and benefits anyone will find if they read through it. Then, you can post the video along with the link. Not everything on LinkedIn has to be video. Text posts are also very valuable.

The opening sentence of your text post should lead with a perfect opening sentence that acts as the hook to read more. This hook should be attention-grabbing but also clearly present the content's major goal. If the hook does this well, it will be clear to the reader why they need to embrace and read the rest of the content. What makes a good hook? Something captivating and pattern-breaking, punchy, and maybe even a little controversial.

Leveraging Your Team

Finally, you should consider leveraging your entire team for distribution. Encourage them to share content that the company has published. Run internal, incentive-based competitions where the post on LinkedIn with the most engagement earns some kind of bonus, like a trip for two. Fun, quirky team-building activities bent around LinkedIn distribution can ultimately increase the brand visibility on the channel. It can also inspire your team to think strategically and find innovative ways to leverage the channel, thus gaining them skills to grow their own career.

You might be thinking, *What if members on my team do such a good job amplifying content, they get a bunch of new job offers?* Sorry to say, these are good problems to have. Presumably, your team's strength is derived, in part, from your leadership. If organizations want your people, it means you have created a culture where people grow and become their best selves. That means entry-level workers will want to work for you. But, as your organization grows, you will also have the opportunity to raise wages to retain them.

Case Study: Gong

Gong is one of the most successful companies at leveraging LinkedIn to drive meaningful business results. The company generates 7.4 million visits a year through LinkedIn and has 75,000 subscribers. Over the last few years, they've become a household name among sales reps. Gong is a tool that essentially listens to your conversations, uses AI to analyze those conversations, and then offers guidance on how to improve your sales techniques.

One thing Gong does extremely well—their secret sauce, if you will—is the creation of engaging, emotionally driven visuals. When you look at their published articles, the graphics and visuals do the speaking for Gong and help guide the user into an understanding of what's to come. The visuals of a Gong ad make it difficult to scroll past, especially after you've engaged with the brand. The Gong teams understand the power of using engaging emotion in their graphics. The brand lived this by featuring photos of famous tech giants Steve Jobs and Steve Ballmer surrounded by their branded colors and in one photo with the letters ROI pho-toshopped to be coming out of their mouth.

The graphics are very consistent, demonstrating an understanding of branding. In the user's mind, a pattern begins to emerge: Gong articles will feature purple, pink, and an image of a person. If a user enjoys Gong's content, they won't need to carefully look at each post on LinkedIn. They can scroll until they see purply pink.

Second, the visuals stop the user in their tracks. They feature things that the audience, Gongsters as they are called, care about deeply. Jobs and Balmer are two iconic individuals in the world of sales. Further, projecting "ROI" out of Jobs' mouth calls attention to the return on invest-ment that all salespeople are thinking about. By putting "ROI" in the mouth of an industry icon, the user is more apt to believe credible information will follow.

As you cultivate your own presence on LinkedIn, find your voice and branding in such a manner that, like Gong, makes you instantly recognizable while demonstrating your value to your audience.

Stay on Top of Changes

LinkedIn's execution difficulty hovers somewhere around seven out of ten. It's a somewhat isolated platform, and you can't parlay your work there onto other platforms easily. Further, things on LinkedIn change frequently. This includes both its overall format as well as what users prefer in their consumption conventions. It seems odd that users would have their tastes change quickly, but LinkedIn is known for experimenting with different formats and channels while guiding users into new trends. So, you need to be on top of what trends and types of content people actually want on LinkedIn.

X (TWITTER) STRATEGIES

- **Goal**: Generate referral traffic from X to your content or product.
- **Difficulty Rating**: 9/10

When news breaks, it breaks on X. Over the course of my adult life, there hasn't been a social network that has acted as the primary vehicle for delivering news to users the way Twitter/X has. It is, without question, one of the most fascinating channels that exists.

It was one of the first fully open channels. While LinkedIn stayed limited to professionals and Facebook stayed limited to those with a university email address, Twitter was always a place where anybody could connect, converse, or argue with folks on the other side of the world.

X can be a divisive place. Do some people hate it? Of course. Do some people love it? No doubt. At the end of the day, X is a channel where anyone can curate their own experience if they follow the right people. I'm in the camp of still getting a ton of value out of X. It's still a money channel for me. It might be a ghost channel in a few years (I doubt it). For now, it can ring the cash register. If you create and share the right content, you can live in a bubble where you are exclusively able to stay focused on what your goals are for this channel. This bubble dynamic and opportunity is actually what makes X so good.

I'll go personal for a bit. X has connected me with clients with multibillion-dollar market caps that have signed million-dollar deals with my company. Some of these clients start by just following me on X (@TheCoolestCool). As they consume my content and we build rapport and trust, they reach out to me about how my team can help their team unlock new opportunities for growth. At least once every other week, I hear from a founder or marketer at a publicly traded cloud company looking to learn more about Foundation because they follow me on Twitter or saw a thread I shared. The return on investment of my X content and the distribution it offers our company is significant and growing every single day. My hope is that in this section you will learn techniques that allow you to surpass even me.

Distribution on X happens in three key ways. One is your bio, which gives you the opportunity to add a link to your website or product. Second is in the tweets themselves. You can share videos, promote links, upload images, and put most of your content there in your format of choice. The third is through other people's tweets. If somebody sends a tweet asking for recommendations on something that a ready-made piece of your content answers, then post your content in reply. Or you can simply build an audience by replying to people who have bigger yet similar audiences with value-packed content.

Like almost every channel, your first goal with X is to drive traffic to your content or product. The secondary goal is to build a following to consistently grow engagement with your X-based content. This following, once built, is where you start to see distribution come easy.

X Bio

Your bio is a digital billboard. Your profile needs to be worth following and optimized to tell your story. Potential followers will look over your X bio much the same way folks look over the bios of possible partners on a dating app. When someone looks at your bio for the first time, they need to quickly understand if what they're getting themselves into by following you is something they think is worthwhile. It's like the sizing up that happens during a handshake.

Most X users are not a household name. You might be among that group. So, when someone visits your X account, it needs to act as a billboard that delivers essential information in a succinct and engaging way. It's your opportunity to tell them everything that they need to know about why they should follow you, what you're about, and who you are.

Your bio is not a time to be humble. The bio, links, your profile picture, and your pinned tweet are all something that accomplish the specific job of selling yourself. Why should a complete stranger smash that follow button? It's your job to ensure your bio makes that answer clear to them.

Your bio should focus on your accomplishments and achievements. This helps other users understand why you are an authority on a specific topic and gives you a sense of credibility in your industry. Additionally, you want to talk about what you use X for. What do you post about? If you visit my X account, @TheCoolestCool, it might still say "Tweeting about SaaS, marketing and growth while watching Fresh Prince of Bel Air reruns or Eagles football."

My bio does two key things. One, it educates people on the content that I tweet about. Two, it gives people a glimpse into what I care about as a human. *Fresh Prince of Bel Air* and the NFL are two touchstone elements of pop culture that may connect me with potential followers. Additionally, I reference the fact that I am a CEO, giving additional credibility.

Figure 8.1

My pinned tweet is also intentional. It presents a rhetorical and engaging question about X strategy. Presumably, my followers or would-be followers have strategies of their own, making it ripe for engagement and comments. Furthermore, by offering my own strategy, I demonstrate my marketing expertise. This tweet helps set the standard for what value potential followers can expect from my account while staying human in the process.

At the time of writing, my pinned tweet has over 200,000 impressions, meaning that it has shown up in people's feeds that many times. For one simple tweet, 200,000 brains saw my content and had an opportunity to continue to engage in my content and possibly reach out to me as a client. Enough said. Twitter is a powerful tool to reach an audience.

X (Formerly Known as Twitter) Content

As promised, it will be useful to return to the Four E's. As they pertain uniquely to X, you need to make your tweets engaging, educational, entertaining, and empowering. Regardless of how you are mixing these attributes, keep in mind that Twitter offers you the option to send a one-off tweet or create a Twitter thread, which is a long-form series of tweets that are connected to one another.

ENGAGING

On X, an engaging tweet is almost literal. That means that the tweet should somehow solicit participation from the user reading your content. For example, you might share five of your favorite books you've read this year. But at the end of that tweet, you could encourage users to reply with their own favorites.

The easiest way to get engagement on X is by asking questions. From the example discussed, that question might read like this: "What are your five favorite books of this past year?"

EDUCATIONAL

If you want to make meaningful educational content on X, it should break down the key takeaways the user needs to know. Depending on how in-depth you want to get with your educational elements, consider using a thread to string together the details and nuance.

ENTERTAINING

In terms of growing your X followers, entertaining tweets are your bread and butter. Whether it's a meme, a random thought, or something that leaves people inspired, people on X love this stuff. How can you test whether or not a tweet is entertaining? By applying the golden (grinning) rule: would it make someone smile?

EMPOWERING

X empowerment comes in the form of showing other handles (or other accounts) love. Tell your followers that they would benefit from following other people. Celebrate people who you love to follow in your tweets. Give them retweets. Promote other people's work. That positive comradery will build a meaningful connection, and your followers will benefit from this type of content at large.

Consistency Is Key

The difficulty of leveraging X to create a great distribution channel is a nine out of ten. Why is it so difficult? X requires consistency. AI tools and ghostwriters are making this easier today, but it's still not easy to grow a high-quality audience on Twitter. You need to frequently and regularly produce content to be successful. Everyone starts with zero followers on X. Scaling up to hundreds of thousands of genuine followers usually takes time. You have to embrace and understand that your tweets need to be varied and come regularly. Only through regular and engaging tweets can you build up a following and drive traffic from your Twitter account to your website.

The best part about X is that, if your audience is engaged, you can send a tweet in less than a minute and, only moments later, hundreds of people have clicked and started consuming your content or product. Don't ignore the possibilities of the power of one tweet.

FACEBOOK STRATEGIES

- **Goal**: Drive referral traffic from Facebook to your content, links, or product.
- **Difficulty Rating**: 8/10

Facebook has redefined what social media means for society. It's polarizing, to be sure, but it was the first channel to reach a billion users. Since its launch in 2004 to the publication of this book, it has been one of the most influential channels in the world.

Some people love it. Some people hate it. They both have good reasons. In any case, the ability to influence people on Facebook is significant. One piece of content can spread and reach millions of people in a matter of seconds on this channel. It can change the way people operate, act, and even vote. You may even have people in your life that constantly begin their stories with the sentence "I read on Facebook..." almost as much (if not more) than they say something like "I heard on the news..."

Its influence cannot be understated. And for that reason, Facebook is a distribution channel that every organization should use with the primary goal of driving referral traffic from the platform to your content, website, or product. Get your links on Facebook clicked!

Facebook Content

Once again, the Four *E*'s will be your best friend in creating excellent Facebook content. How do you bend each of those four concepts around Facebook-specific conventions? Let's find out.

ENGAGING

Brands on Facebook use quite a few strategies to generate engaging posts. One of the most common is the "call to action" concept, an evolution of the "this or that" concept. Think of Twix posting an image of their famous candy bar. They are currently running a marketing campaign where each of the two bars that comes in a single package has been deemed either the Left Twix or Right Twix. A Facebook update could easily offer a call to action: "Does the user prefer Left or Right Twix?" Those following the brand will feel tempted to engage.

Something else that creates strong engagement is often called Newsjacking, which I prefer to call reactive storytelling. This means a big story is making the rounds, and your post is able to make that story relevant to your branding, content, or marketing message. Companies like LADbible do this brilliantly.

Content that is highly emotional does extremely well on Facebook. Name the emotion. Joy. Nostalgia. Outrage. Surprise. Desire. If you create an update that articulates an emotion clearly, strongly, and in a way that aligns with your content or branding, you are likely to create engagement.

EDUCATIONAL

It might seem like Facebook doesn't offer much opportunity for educational experiences other than an embedded link to a news website. But that couldn't be further from reality. Many brands are sharing educational content in the form of DIY information. That might be a how-to video, a recipe, craft activities, or any other educational genre that can be seen and understood from a quick glance.

Facebook is also a place where people go to be informed on news and information. Most of the time, these are embedded or linked elements and are not directly produced on Facebook. Nonetheless, if there is educational content that you've created or found elsewhere, you can embed it in a status update to share with your audience.

ENTERTAINING

Facebook provides you the opportunity to create targeted fun surrounding the narrative of your content or product. Because you have established a clear online and social media presence, your audience should have certain expectations of you. You can make your content more entertaining if you put a clever and funny spin on these expectations.

Let's look at an example. Let's say you're a marketer for a chain restaurant and are looking to promote a new ribs entre during an international soccer tournament. You could post an image of this ribs meal with a caption that reads "Eat your ribs soccer style: with no hands."

EMPOWERING

Facebook can empower users in several ways, and you can be the brand that helps them feel empowered. One of the most common ways to do this on Facebook is to start a donation fund for an important cause. Not only does this show your followers what type of person you are, it also helps any donors feel like they are contributing to a worthwhile cause. By virtue of you empowering them to make a donation, they feel a connection to your brand.

Another opportunity for empowerment is contests. If your organization is large enough, you can post chances to win prizes, like gift cards or brand-related merchandise. Although the user is empowered to participate, this also falls under the "engaging" moniker, as it tends to encourage user engagement.

Page vs. Profile vs. Group

When starting a Facebook account for yourself or your organization, the crucial first question is whether or not you will be creating a Page, a Profile, or a Group. Pages are used for businesses or brands. Profiles are used for individuals. And Groups are used to generate a community of users centered around some topic or shared interest.

PAGE

Facebook Pages themselves are the king of "likes". (Note: You need a Profile in order to establish a Page.) The expectation is that the administrator is acting on behalf of the organization or entity. These are curated spaces, much like a website, where the entity can display content for and interact with fans or customers.

People who follow a Page are interested in hearing what it has to offer regarding the organization or brand it represents. The follower's expectation is that the content on this page (and any updates that hit the feed) are more informational and content-based. That is a different expectation than a Profile. Profiles are meant to catalog and list a series of small status updates.

PROFILE

The Facebook Profile is where a monolithic feed appears. The Profile owner can share information about themselves in the form of status updates. That might mean saying a little bit about oneself in a text post, sharing photos or videos, or "checking in" on places they're visiting and enjoying. There is a "Professional Mode" to profiles that helps individual content creators cultivate their branding to their followers.

GROUP

Facebook Groups act as private communities where users connect one-to-one. They can vary in size, but some can be quite large, with numbers in excess of millions of users. (Note: You need a Facebook Profile to join or manage a Group.)

Regardless of size, Groups are much more intimate than Pages or Profiles because they are invite-only. That means the followers of a Group are all interested in the same ideas. If you are a member of a Group interested in a topic aligned with your content, your posts will have more valuable engagements. I will cover Facebook Groups in more detail in Chapter 10.

Acquiring Facebook Audiences

One of my favorite techniques to grow Facebook followers is simply to acquire someone's inactive Facebook Page. I call these graveyard Facebook Pages.

Pages have been around since 2007. I don't know about you, but my life has changed quite a bit since 2007. For me, there's been three kids and a smattering of gray hair. It's unclear if the gray hair is from the kids or the age. The jury is still out—but I digress. The reality is that there are many Facebook Pages that have been around for a long time and are now graveyards.

Pick the topic. There is likely a graveyard Page about it. Engineering. Plant-based food. Sales. Artificial intelligence. There are unused Facebook Pages with thousands upon thousands of followers. Reach out to the administrators of these Pages and set to acquire them to become the new administrator.

For example, I own another company that is dedicated to plant-based food and recipes. (Don't ask. I like to diversify my investments.) I quickly identified a graveyard Facebook Page with over 80,000 followers, offered the administrator $5,000, and, after acquisition, began promoting this company's content on the Facebook Page. Within weeks, the company had made its money back and then some on the back of a following that had already been created.

Facebook Pages or Groups that are collecting dust can shortcut your way to increased audience size. A following that could take months or years to build could be yours instantly.

An Offbeat Algorithm

Successful distribution on Facebook has a difficulty rating of eight out of ten. The primary reason? The algorithm changes quickly and rapidly. You never know when the structure of the algorithm will change or why. This changing system means that you need to always be alert for the content expectations and, in some cases, even the mode of content delivery.

INSTAGRAM STRATEGIES

- **Goal**: From Instagram, send your target audience to your content, website, or product.
- **Difficulty Rating**: 9/10

A visual-first platform, Instagram was originally created for posting photos. It has grown beyond that. Now, you can share videos, Stories, status updates, reels, long-form content, and more. It's a place for rich content—on Instagram you have the opportunity to connect with your audience in a meaningful way, to further distribute your content.

As is often the case, your primary goal with Instagram is to drive traffic toward your content, website, or product. The secondary goal is to use this channel as a branding device to build your following and let users know what kind of content you create.

Instagram Bio

Like with Twitter, make sure you view your Instagram Bio and Profile as a billboard or handshake. The user will get their first impression of you, your content, and your brand by interacting with this Bio. It needs to be representative of why you are worth following.

You can "Pin to Your Profile" with Instagram content. Pinned content should be relevant to your target audience and among the best content you've produced. Look at your Instagram analytics, and pin the pieces that have the most likes and shares.

Use a memorable Profile picture, something that's iconic and represents your brand or image. If you're an organization, your logo is a good place to start. Like a logo itself, a Profile picture is meant to leave a lasting impression on your followers as they consume your content in other mediums and channels.

The Bio content is the most important step in creating a first impression. You have 200 characters to tell the world why your Instagram page is worth following and what you offer as a brand. Additionally, you have a chance to encourage users to share content relevant to your brand using a specific hashtag. With that in mind, here are four things to include in your Instagram Bio:

- **Hashtags**: #BrandName
- **Your slogan or brand's voice**: Just Do It
- **Call to action**: Click the link in our bio
- **Emojis**: 💯

If it makes sense for your situation, consider also including your email or contact information, so people know how to get in touch with you. Along the same lines, add a mobile-friendly URL to your website so followers can easily reach your other content. To do this, use a tool like LinkTree or Beacons. The point is to drive your followers down the path to purchase or content consumption as much as possible.

Story Highlights

Directly underneath the Bio is an area for Story Highlights. These short videos or timed images give you an opportunity to further tell your brand's story. The great thing about Story Highlights is it centralizes some of your best content in one place. Videos, blog posts, and your other greatest hits can be housed here. Highlight what's important to you and what will drive return on investment for your business.

For this feature, curate things that are relative to your target audience. If, for example, you are targeting salespeople, a Highlight video could be dedicated to tips, another to behind-the-scenes work that creates a connection with your brand, and a third that is about your personal life to connect users to you. Each of these three can mention different pieces of content you've created for the sales-based followers to consume on your website or elsewhere.

If you are uncertain about how to edit and create Story Highlight videos, I encourage you to download a separate app dedicated to helping you create Stories videos.

Instagram Content

There are a variety of strategies to consider when creating Instagram content. Each specific strategy can be housed within one of the handy, dandy Four *E*'s.

ENGAGING

Perhaps the most engaging form of storytelling unique to Instagram is behind-the-scenes content. Showing the inner workings of an organization, brand, or person authenticates the Instagram profile as being sincere. Behind-the-scenes posts demonstrate that you are interested in connection above consumption. That connection makes your followers feel engaged and like you are speaking directly to them.

Another engaging side effect of behind-the-scenes content is folks are generally interested in how things are made. Think *How It's Made*, the long-running documentary series showing how manufactured goods are made. If a microbrew posts a video about how they make their beer, followers are more likely to feel the local connection being involved with the success of that company. This type of content can be engaging and powerful.

One of my biggest overall pieces of advice on succeeding with Instagram is to look at the Discover page to find the most popular elements of competitor content. Search the keywords relevant to your industry. Why? Carousels, reels, and posts that have traction will start populating, and you can get inspiration from them.

EDUCATIONAL

For Instagram, an educational piece should be indirect. Your Instagram post, story, or update directs your followers to the fact that you have a new piece of educational content that has gone live. Your post's caption (or the image itself) can refer users to a link in your Bio that will then send them to the content in question.

If you are posting a video directing them to the educational content, I encourage you to use some kind of consistent, on-brand visual presentation.

ENTERTAINING

If we're being honest, Instagram is a meme machine. People love sending the memes they find on Instagram to the DMs of their besties. They're hilarious and hugely entertaining. Sometimes, these entertaining exchanges of content are what hold long-term or long-distance relationships together.

Meme-based storytelling is when brands leverage a popular meme and use it to communicate a brand-relevant message. Whether it's the Dos Equis guy or the "Hey Girl" meme with Ryan Gosling, even the most boring brands can succeed using meme-based storytelling to stand out.

Memes are their own little niche of pop culture, and pop culture is an attention hog. Our collective obsession with it is the reason why businesses like TMZ and BuzzFeed generate millions of visits on a regular basis. Interweaving pop culture into your Instagram content is a great opportunity for you to connect with your audience using something top-of-mind they can relate to or are passionate about.

Part and parcel of entertaining content is a great caption. Great captions will let the follower self-identify, meaning they can quickly discern from the caption whether or not it pertains to their interests or pain points.

You should also use hashtags. With hashtags, less is more because humans don't speak in them. Pick a handful of hashtags that might send the followers to more content they love.

EMPOWERING

Sparking emotions in your target audience is the most effective way to drive shares, likes, comments, and any sort of connection to your brand. Studies show that the more powerful the emotion, the more likely the user will react to the content.

One way to empower your followers through emotional methods is to use inspiring and motivational quotes. Whether or not those quotes are attributed to famous people or experts in their field doesn't matter quite as much as the quote itself. But make no mistake, an inspirational quote from Albert Einstein generally carries more weight than a quote from your co-worker, Dave Random-Mann.

Another form of empowerment is what is sometimes called "like bait." On Facebook, that takes the form of "like this status update if you love Fridays!" On Instagram, the equivalent would be telling the follower to "double tap." Tapping a photo twice on Instagram triggers the like response. By encouraging followers to engage with the content itself, you offer them an opportunity to use their voice—a form of empowerment—to help shape the brand.

Third-Party Accounts

One of the best ways to grow an account on Instagram is through other people's accounts. If you have 100 followers and another account has 100,000, it's going to benefit you greatly to have them amplify and share your handle with their followers. We've embraced this strategy at my company, Hustle & Grind, to grow the @HustleGrindCo Instagram account to over 100,000 followers. You can do this by simply finding accounts with a similar audience as you and offering to either pay for a shoutout or exchange a shoutout for a shoutout. The idea of a "shoutout" is simply them putting up a post that talks about you and why their followers should check out your account.

Hard Landing

It's very difficult to encourage somebody using Instagram to leave the app and visit a website, because people are there to consume in-app content. The difficulty rating for leveraging Instagram for distribution is a nine out of ten. Users want to see pictures, watch videos, share memes, and continue to scroll through to the pieces of content that capture their attention. If we're talking about video content or image content, it's easy. If it's text-related, good luck. The typical Instagram user is not interested in scrolling through their curated content in order to click on a hyperlink and find themselves on a landing page. It's just not what users do at the moment. It can be difficult to distribute your work, considering Instagram users want a very specific experience.

TIKTOK STRATEGIES

- **Goal**: From the app, send referral traffic back to your website, content, or product. Secondarily, build your audience on this platform to increase referrals.
- **Difficulty Rating**: 10/10

Relative to other social media platforms, TikTok is innovative in its use of short-form videos. Its original presentational format was so unique that many other platforms are starting to copy their features. Beyond revolutionizing the way that video content is consumed, created, and spread, the app itself has a ton of functionality. You can shoot, edit, and post interesting content without ever leaving the TikTok platform.

TikTok is not talked about often as a business channel outside of B2C, which is a distribution strategy that can be difficult to build. However, there is an opportunity for businesses of all types on TikTok, especially if you're trying to connect with a younger demographic. This is especially important if the business hopes to build a long relationship with its target audience, increasing their lifetime value for its brand, product, or content.

Like many other channels, your goals with TikTok are to drive traffic back to your website or content and to build up a following within the platform itself in order to tap into that audience in the future. Users and TikTok traffic starts with an interaction with your profiles, which is exactly where you should start.

Note: TikTok comes with a lot of risk. It's a channel that is here today but could be gone tomorrow depending on whether or not the political climate in your country is pro-TikTok or anti-TikTok.

Profile Optimization

On TikTok, it's important for people to click on your account profile to get to know you. TikTok's profile is very similar to the other channels. You want to tell followers about yourself, such as your interests, your profession, and what they can expect from your TikTok content. Perhaps more so than other platforms, nearly all TikTok bios feature an emoji, so pick an emoji that is fun, unique, but somehow appropriately related to your profile content. And you need to add a call to action that directs followers to a link.

TikTok users want to stay on the platform and are resistant to clicking on anything that will send them off of it. Nonetheless, the only real way to drive traffic from your account to your content is to provide links in your bio. Hopefully, your other profile-optimization work (and your content itself) is enough to convince the follower to click on that link and continue to consume your content on other channels.

Leverage Other People's Content

It's difficult to drive traffic from TikTok, but that doesn't mean it's impossible. How can you generate traffic beyond profile optimization? Leverage TikTok influencers by engaging them. Can you identify influencers who are creating highly valuable content on TikTok today? Many may have large swaths of followers that are your target audience. You should look for influencers within your industry's space who can amplify and promote your content or product. Reach out to these individuals and ask if they can be a brand ambassador or partner.

Similarly, perhaps you can sponsor them or give them a free product in exchange for featuring that product in their TikTok content. Obviously, you would want to work with this individual to ensure any content they create with you is aligned with your own understanding of your target audience.

High-Value Content

If you do embrace the idea of creating content from scratch on TikTok, it's important to embrace the Sherlock Homeboy Method. Begin studying the way in which people are currently consuming content on TikTok and how it differs from what is consumed on other channels like YouTube. Reverse-engineer the content you see by putting on the Homeboy hat.

As you begin to consume high-value content on TikTok, you'll see a pattern of selfie-style short videos. The aesthetic resembles a person holding a phone out and pointing it directly back at themselves. They'll simply be talking about something relevant to their audience. These selfie videos are intimate and generate a sense of personal connection with the creator due to the conversational structure.

Another popular TikTok genre to experiment with includes a reaction video. This is where the creators will watch another video about a topic and record themselves reacting to it. Like the early days of the "Let's Play" video game genre, most business-world content creators scoff at the idea of a reaction video and see it as having no value. But the opposite is true. TikTok users quite enjoy this genre. It is social media, after all. It stands to reason that when a follower watches a creator

SOCIAL MEDIA DISTRIBUTION

react to another video, it simulates a connective and social experience.

A reaction video for your purposes might be recording yourself reacting to a news clip or talking head covering content relevant to your industry. Going back to the principle of reactive and emotional storytelling, content that generates more engagement is usually overly emotional. You may want to pick a particularly egregious or incorrect clip and humorously explain a more complete perspective.

The use of audio or music to play over a video is also something wildly popular on TikTok. That means you'll have to do a lot of research about what music is currently trending on TikTok and why. Use popular music in your own videos. Here are some TikTok-commissioned statistics from an analytics company that detail the impact of trending music on TikTok:

- Sixty-seven percent of users want to see TikTok videos from brands that feature trending audio.
- Sixty-eight percent of users say trending audio helps them remember the brand better.
- Fifty-eight percent of users say they're more likely to talk about a brand or share an ad that features trending sounds.

- Sixty-two percent say they're curious to learn about the brand after watching a video with trending sounds.[10]

What becomes almost immediately clear with TikTok is that, more or less, brand guidelines are out the door. When you take up these TikTok-specific genres, it's not a case where you can bend the video formats around your marketing message. Rather, you'll have to bend your message around the platform to get the greatest returns.

Hashtags

For TikTok, hashtags are extremely important because they are supported by the algorithm. The more a specific hashtag is being used in separate pieces of content, the more likely it is to show up in people's feeds.

In order to create effective hashtags, they need to align them with several things. First, they should clearly reflect your content, campaign, or call to action. Further, they should be the same hashtags you have created and use on your other social media channels, creating synergy your

---

10 "New Studies Quantify TikTok's Growing Impact on Culture and Music," *TikTok.com*, July 21, 2021, https://newsroom.tiktok.com/en-us/new-studies-quantify-tiktoks-growing-impact-on-culture-and-music/.

followers recognize. You should use multiple hashtags, but don't inundate your followers with too many. How can you approach that strategically? Using only two or three hashtags total, combine your on-brand-but-niche hashtag with something that is popular or trending. Because the trending hashtags will bring new followers to a piece of content, it will hopefully increase the popularity of your niche hashtag.

Finally, like any good slogan, hashtags should be extremely simple, easy to spell, and easy to share. Don't confuse my comparison to slogans as an indication hashtags need to be a full sentence. Rather, your goal is to make them catchy and memorable. Don't use hashtags that are a half dozen words long, use a commonly misspelled word, or aren't catchy.

Cinematic Practice

TikTok is, undoubtedly, the toughest channel to distribute content successfully unless you're creating native video content for the platform. The one caveat to that bold statement is that any company can run ads on the platform. But in terms of organic video content, my difficulty rating lands at a ten out of ten. The barrier is the fact that TikTok is 100 percent video content. This format is not something traditional marketers are used to working with. Further, driving traffic to your site can be minimal unless you have a viral hit.

REMEMBER: TELL THEM WHAT TO DO

Yes, it's important to create engaging, educational, entertaining, and empowering content in all of your social media channels. But you also need to direct the user where to go next. The call to action is crucial. If you don't tell people to "Click the link in the bio" or "Subscribe to the newsletter" or "Buy one today on my website," it is very unlikely users will engage with your content or product outside the social media platform. Encourage your audience to do something. Guide them to take action to increase the effectiveness of your distribution efforts.

As I've mentioned, part of how you can guide your audience is to include a link in your bio or profile. You have a few different options I want to highlight here. The first link option is a link to your website. Obviously, your ultimate goal is to drive traffic back to your website or content. But leaving a link to your website on every bio can, over time, create a slowdown in traffic due to lack of authenticity. Social media followers want to feel connected to a brand, and a link to a website feels like a connection to a salesperson. So, consider mixing it up with alternatives frequently to make your followers feel like you are curating an experience for them. It's important to give them multiple pathways on their journey to your content. With many paths, the user feels like they've participated in choosing the route.

So, what would other links look like? You could send them to your "About" page instead, helping followers get to know you or the organization better. If you are running a content giveaway or promotion, you can provide a link to the contest rules or discount terms, a sign-up page, or a webpage featuring information about what they stand to win or save (or all three). As it pertains to your specific content or products, you could link to a blog link that pertains to specific news or how-tos in your industry. Or send them to a launch page to generate interest in a new piece of content or product. You could also rotate links directly to your best-selling products or pieces of content with the most engagement. Consider using a link to highlight a free sample of content or demo for your product. Finally, don't forget the importance of cross-pollinating your content distribution. The link could guide users to one of your published articles for a third party, a YouTube video, a podcast, your newsletter, or something else.

Acting as the guide for your followers and frequently pointing them in new directions is vitally important, because social media is constantly changing. But if you can stay on top of your social media game and crack its codes, you unlock an audience of millions and, if you hit a viral spark, billions.

PARTNERSHIP DISTRIBUTION

THERE'S A WELL-KNOWN AND POWERFUL EXPRES-
sion: If you want to go fast, go alone, but if you want to
go far, go together. Partnerships position you to go far.

In the world of business, two brands promoting each other is better than one promoting themselves.
Further still, a promotional collaboration creates a wonderful hybrid of content or product that represents the
strengths of both brands. Need an example? How about
the Doritos Locos Taco from Taco Bell?

Picture the product in your mind. It was a standard Taco Bell Taco, but the shell was flavored like a Dorito Chip. Sounds delicious, right? By collaborating on content and sharing audiences, both collaborators are incentivized to make the campaign a success, increasing traffic or value metrics for each.

Let's illustrate the power of partnership distribution in the world of content marketing. Over 5.6 million people visit *Social Media Examiner* every year. Back in 2015, I recognized this website would become a go-to resource for content marketers and those learning about the marketing industry. It continues to be a space for building skills and gleaning industry insights. In short, the audience of *Social Media Examiner* happened to perfectly align with the audience I wanted to reach.

I made it my mission to establish a partnership with *Social Media Examiner* and tap into their large audience. I reached out to the editorial team, we held some preliminary discussions, and they accepted one of my pieces of content for publication on their site. The content in question was titled "How to Create Instagram Ads." Keep in mind that when this story went live, Instagram was still relatively new, and this piece was topical and of high value to the website's audience, who was looking to crack the code of an increasingly popular social media platform.

Within a matter of minutes, after my piece went live, traffic back to my website and my social media follower counts significantly increased. My brand's recognition and credibility grew, too. It even attracted a number of new clients who remain major pieces of my client portfolio today. All of these positive benefits were the result of partnering with one entity and creating one post in *one* high-traffic area. The lesson I learned was clear: there is tremendous value in partnership distribution. Since this post, I've gone on to partner with dozens of other websites in an effort to continue spreading my content to an audience that finds it valuable.

Whether you are just starting out or are a seasoned distribution veteran, partnerships are a great way to increase the size of your audience, be they subscribers, followers, or any similar metric. Throughout this chapter, you will learn different ways to implement partnership distribution to spread your story and drive meaningful and measurable results. Included in that is how to find the people, brands, and media partners you can collaborate with to unlock more distribution opportunities.

Working with *Social Media Examiner* was one of my first forays into partnership distribution. You can build your own brand on the back of other people's audiences, networks, and channels. There are countless opportunities to collaborate with individuals, publications, websites, or other professional entities. Building partnerships with the right people translates into wins for all parties involved. Whatever the format, your content will be exposed to a new-to-you audience that grows your target audience. In other words, partnership distribution is pure growth.

BASICS OF PARTNERSHIP DISTRIBUTION

By definition, partnership distribution is the act of sharing your content with third parties that have an audience, content topic, or product aligned with your own audience, content, or product. Hopefully, you and the third party have all of these elements aligned. On top of that, the third-party ideally has a large audience (or, at the very least, an audience larger than yours).

When researching what types of collaborators you could partner with, identify opportunities where both parties can win. This should become your basic criteria when evaluating whether or not a possible partnership is worthwhile. You have pretty clear goals for creating a successful distribution strategy—in other words, you are highly aware of your own goals. But have you thought about *their* goals and objectives? Understanding and fulfilling them with your content will be the perfect foot in the door when you reach out for a potential partnership.

With partnership distribution, you look to add another element to your larger distribution engine and increase referral traffic back to your website, content, or product. However, there are some nuanced additional goals that can vary, depending on the type of partnership distribution you are enacting. Those include increasing backlinks (links to your content on others' websites) for search engine optimization (SEO), generating brand awareness, growing your email list or newsletter subscribers, or, if you sell a product, an uptick in sales.

Overall, partnership distribution scores in my difficulty rating system as a nine out of ten. As you are in the early stages of partnership, it can be especially difficult. You may not have an industry reputation, making you a less attractive partner to larger brands. Your lack of connections and experience may prevent you from finding success when reaching out. It's difficult to get partnerships when no one sees the value that you bring to the table. This doesn't mean you shouldn't still try to unlock partnership opportunities. It just means you should avoid shooting for the moon right out of the gate.

Start out by looking to partner with the medium-sized fish rather than the big, uncatchable one. The big fish probably won't bite your lure. Somebody like MrBeast, with 117 million YouTube subscribers, is very unlikely to agree to partnering with you unless you are an influencer in your industry or have a multimillion-dollar check to write him. If you aren't an influencer or lack a big budget, there is almost nothing you can do to add a ton of value to the big fish like MrBeast at this time. So, make sure your partnerships have aligned incentives, so everybody can win together.

If you are in the early stages of your growth, one great way to partner with entities that may be larger than you is to offer some kind of value to them. In fact, this is good business advice in general. When I first wanted to collaborate with LinkedIn, I reached out with a Slideshare presentation (a company they acquired) that I designed. It was absolutely stunning. I spent my own hard money to design a beautiful presentation all about B2B marketing and then reached out to their editor, feeling my piece would help their audience. This was a way for them to showcase their product and set the bar for content excellence. It was my opportunity to reach millions of new people and establish a relationship that would last for years to come. Now, I'm an instructor with LinkedIn Learning and have collaborated with their team multiple times over the years. The takeaway here is simple: carry the burden of doing the hard work and make it difficult for them to refuse. If you offer to make the bigger brand's job easier, they'll be more likely to agree to the partnership.

Partnerships themselves can range from hosting webinars to contributing a guest blog post. While the possibilities are indeed endless, I will cover my favorite—and the most powerful—partnership strategies and opportunities that can become part of a larger, successful distribution strategy.

STRATEGY 1: JOINT WEBINAR PARTNERSHIP

- **Goal**: Generate referral traffic through backlinks, email subscribers, and sales.
- **Difficulty Rating**: 9/10

Webinars are real-time, online presentations. The allure of a webinar is having direct access to the host, which means possible conversation exchanges or opportunities to ask questions. Joint webinars are typically hosted by organizations looking to provide value to other audiences, companies, or individuals.

Finding webinars is a cinch. Every single day, there are thousands of webinars hosted on the internet. Many are held in professional spaces such as LinkedIn, others behind closed doors through software like GoToWebinar, where people sign up for specific webinars to become educated on a new product, service, piece of technology, or trends within an industry, virtually.

Who uses webinars? Some brands use webinars frequently as part of their own distribution or sales engine to get leads and establish authority. How do you identify eligible partners for joint webinars? Research companies that use webinars, get significant traction from them, and are aligned with your ideal audience. When you identify these brands, reach out to see if they would be interested in you hosting one of their ongoing webinar series and promise them that you will make it worthwhile.

One such aligned partnership occurred in 2022 between my company, Foundation Marketing, and Wix, a website-building software company. We conducted a joint webinar. Wix generates $1.2 billion in revenue a year and has 420,000 followers on Twitter alone. In other words, not only do they create an in-demand product, they also have built up their brand awareness. It's very likely that my ideal-but-untapped audience follows Wix, so when they asked me to partner with them on a webinar, it was a no-brainer to agree.

Through my webinar, I hosted their audience and, by virtue of their vast following, increased my brand awareness while detailing the services of my businesses. I gave both Wix and their audience value in the sense they received content that mattered to them, and I *received* value by unlocking a new audience in my distribution strategy. Like all ideal partnership distributions, both Wix and Foundation increased their audience—a win-win.

Or, consider the folks at Audiense, a social media research software that specializes in audience research. They embraced joint webinars as a partnership distribution strategy with influential marketers in the industry. Their joint webinars are beneficial for both marketers like myself and Audiense, as they gain exposure to my audience and I gain exposure to theirs. Another win-win.

By inviting a marketer who has their own established following onto the webinar, both they and the marketer (in the case above, me) can capture new audiences and are able to grow by talking about already-developed content.

These are no-brainer efforts to increase reach for both entities.

Note: Improv Skills Required

The goals of a joint webinar are to increase traffic back to your website or content (especially if the content can drive new leads), use brand awareness to add subscribers to email lists and newsletters, and possibly increase sales outputs (if applicable). How hard is it to achieve these goals? I give it a difficulty rating of nine out of ten. There is a surprising amount of work and unique skill that goes into hosting a webinar, some of which is not within the realm of the common content marketer's skillsets.

Webinars are, to a large extent, performative. The audience watching in real-time will be huge, creating a unique form of performative pressure. You have to be present and charismatic. You have to be genuine, display empathy and likability, and be able to improvise on the spot. You will receive questions and participate in conversations where uncomfortable or difficult topics will arise. Are you prepared to answer the tough and unexpected questions on the fly? Can you cultivate a professionally charismatic attitude? These are unique skills required for successful joint webinars.

My advice is to attend webinars yourself, put on your Sherlock Homeboy hat, and discern which successful webinars to borrow your structure from.

STRATEGY 2: DISTRIBUTION THROUGH AGGREGATORS

- **Goal**: Generate referral traffic to your content.
- **Difficulty Rating**: 2/10

Aggregators are websites or apps that pull the most recent articles, essays, YouTube videos, podcasts, or other content

mediums and distribute them through their own ecosys-
tems. Typically, each aggregator will work within one
medium or file type. For example, Spotify is an aggregation
platform that delivers audio content (music and podcasts).
Through aggregation and its algorithm, Spotify suggests
and delivers the user's preferred content based on their
interests and prior engagement. These types of sites exist
for other formats beyond music as well like blog posts,
podcasts, and YouTube videos.

Over the years, aggregators have seen a decrease in traction, especially in text-based mediums such as blog posts
(RIP Google Reader). The success of audio and video aggregators has plateaued, and it's unclear if they, like their text
counterparts, will decrease in popularity or remain at their
current demand. For the time being, aggregators are still
a decent resource for distribution. Why? Because lots of
busy, high-value individuals—people worth your attention—
depend on a curated online experience through aggregators.

Relative to your content or product industry, you need
to research the top aggregators that your target audience
is likely to utilize. Two popular aggregation tools are Pocket
and Feedly. Users of these tools can customize their sug-
gested content by selecting and curating their "Followed"
topics. From there, users can bookmark and store content they value to read later in ways that are far more

accessible—such as on a mobile device, even if the original content is not mobile-friendly. The name "Pocket" derives from this read-it-on-the-go feature. Many business people in your target audience will be on the go a lot, so it's likely they curate their online experience through Pocket or a similar app.

The difficulty of using aggregator websites or apps is rated as a two out of ten. Generally, seeding your content for aggregators is very easy: you just set it and forget it. But, as mentioned, you need to find the aggregators that are relevant to your industry. That will take some internet sleuthing on your part but not a tremendous amount.

STRATEGY 3: GUEST BLOG POSTS

- **Goal**: Generate referral traffic to your content and backlinks.
- **Difficulty Rating**: 8/10

The terms used for each of the partnership distribution strategies thus far have their definitions embedded in said terms. But "Guest Blog Posts" takes the cake for ease of understanding. As the term suggests, guest blog posts are blog posts you post as a guest on a third-party site. (I've covered basic blog-post strategies in Chapter 5.) I don't want to be repetitive with the power of blogging, but I do want to offer some basic strategies that are unique to *guest* blog posting.

Your first priority is to find a blog worthy of your contribution. How can you find a worthy blog? Open Google and type in the best blogs in your industry. Seriously. That's it. If you want to get really strategic with the approach you can use a keyword research tool or social media research tool to better understand the audience but a basic Google Search could help set you on your way. Use this research to discern what blogs to send a guest blog post to.

After you've found a few blogs you want to contribute to, it becomes another challenge to reach out to establish a real partnership. The good news is that most blog posts will tell you on their site if they accept guest blog posts or not. As you start going through the research, you'll notice, at the bottom of the website, links for "Contact Us" or "Write For Us." These are the cues to find contact information for their content or editorial boards. Most likely, you will see contact information for a person who leads the guest contribution for the platform (usually an editor). At that point, all you need to do is reach out. Here is a template email you can use as a springboard for your own communications with a targeted blog.

201

Good afternoon, [first name of contact]

I'm a big fan of [insert blog here]. In fact, I've been a reader for quite some time, but I've also been a writer for *X* number of years. Over the last few years, I've written about topics like [insert topics of published work relevant to blog here] and have published content that I think your readers would find valuable.

Here are three pieces I consider to be my best work and representative of what I can produce for your blog.

- [Title of piece #1, hyperlink to content]
- [Title of piece #2, hyperlink to content]
- [Title of piece #3, hyperlink to content]

I would love to contribute to your website, and I believe [one of your listed articles] would generate a lot of value for your audience. What do you think?

Cheers,
[Your first name]

With the blog found and the partnership brokered, it's time to write.

The power of using guest blog posts as a channel is fueled by the post you publish. First, I recommend including references to other content directly in your guest piece. Be as direct or indirect as the guest website's rules or conventions allow. Being direct might mean dropping the name of your other piece of content or embedding your other content. Being indirect might mean hyperlinking an inconspicuous phrase back to your content.

If you are able to, embed your other content into your guest blog post. Make sure that content is highly relevant to the information in your guest blog post but also information the audience would find valuable. For example, if you write a guest post about Instagram best practices and also have a YouTube video on the same topic, then you can embed that content into the guest post itself. This simple technique could help your YouTube traffic increase by thousands of views.

Many people think guest posts are just for SEO purposes only. They'll post content in all sorts of places with a plethora of links but no audience at all. This kind of execution stands a chance of gaining you little-to-no traction *and* damaging your reputation. Be careful.

Directing Traffic

The power of guest blog posting is only accessible if you are able to use a larger audience to direct traffic back to your site or content. If you write a great guest blog post for a website with a huge following, your own reach will increase. If you embed additional content into that post, that growth potential increases, too.

Never forget: guest blogging is about referral traffic and reach above all else. Partially for that reason, it can be rather difficult to succeed at, earning an eight out of ten difficulty rating. The difficulty really comes from the fact that you will have to write a new piece of content. Some of the lessons you learned in the remixing and republishing chapters will be available to you here. But more than anything, you will have to hunker down, use your creative skills, and give something amazing to an audience that isn't yours (yet).

Overall, guest blogging creates connections that could lead to life-changing experiences and revenue for your business.

STRATEGY 4: PRODUCT AND PLATFORM DISTRIBUTION

- **Goal:** Generate sales of your product or service.
- **Difficulty Rating:** 9/10

- **Disclaimer**: This section only applies to readers looking to distribute a *product*. Those who distribute content only will find this strategy does not apply to them.

Product and platform distribution can be extremely powerful for scaling sales of a product. This strategy is the process of listing your product on an online distribution platform, such as the Apple App Store for iPhone users. For another option, if you want to generate revenue (or even exposure) from your podcasts, you could think about listing your podcasts on Spotify. If you have a SaaS product that integrates with Salesforce, you could list it on the Salesforce app exchange, immediately unlocking the distribution power of the Salesforce ecosystem. If you have an e-commerce tool that works with Shopify stores, you can leverage the Shopify App Store.

What makes product and platform distribution so attractive is the platforms themselves are usually perfectly aligned with the audience you are trying to reach. It gets you in front of the right people and taps into a massive distribution network that is often overlooked. So many e-commerce stores will place themselves only on Etsy, eBay, or another platform to access buyers. But what if you could also create an app that lives on the user's iPhone and lets them make purchases from your e-commerce store? This often overlooked strategy could very quickly pay major dividends.

Products come in all shapes and sizes, even if many are entirely digital. What may apply to your situation is so diverse that I can't really go beyond what's written here. Identify what platforms in your product's space could be harnessed for baked-in distribution with your product. You will have to gauge which platforms speak best to both the distribution you're looking for but also how that platform reflects on your brand.

The Business of Distribution

Product and platform distribution skews more heavily into the business world than it does to the distribution world. Therefore, the difficult rating comes in at nine out of ten. You need to have a clear, thoughtful, and professional handle on your own sales engine and business plan. Then, you have to decide if you can acquire customers through these platforms aligned with your plans. Is your website built in a way that can be self-serviced? Is your product built in a way where somebody could acquire it through an app? If not, do you have the resources to hire the engineers or team needed to better use these platforms? At this rate, product and platform distribution can balloon into a full-blown go-to-market strategy rather than a simple distribution one. However, if your product happens to already be an app or podcast, this won't be as difficult for you.

The only other obstacle you face is adhering to the guidelines of the platform. Follow them.

STRATEGY 5: NEWSLETTER PARTNERSHIP

- **Goal**: Generate referral traffic back to your content or website, increase sales, and increase brand awareness.
- **Difficulty Rating**: 9/10

I've spoken about newsletters and their partnerships to some degree already, so you should have some basic knowledge. But to recap, newsletters are the digital equivalent of direct mail. Nobody likes spam, but people do love emails that are valuable and cater to their specific needs. In theory, newsletters do just that. And because of that value, subscribers will sign up for newsletters to curate their own email experience with weekly insights and information relevant to them.

Don't forget: most folks hardly ever change their email addresses. That means when they sign up for a newsletter, they will be receiving that content for life. This makes

newsletter partnerships a particularly valuable distribution channel, especially if your content is seeded in a
high-volume newsletter aligned with your audience.

Identify the newsletters that are prominent in your
space. Use your regular keywords in your research, except
include "newsletter" as one of them. You will be met with
a handful of different blog posts talking about the newsletters various CEOs, CFOs, and CIOs in your content area
read. Some might even reveal the newsletters popular
with practitioners, not just the leaders, of your content
industry. Once you've found the right ones, subscribe to
them and read them. Assess whether or not they would be
relevant to your audience.

As you reach out to the folks who run these newsletters
for partnership, there are one of three ways it could go.
First, consider sponsorship, where you cut a check to seed
your content in their next newsletter, including the strategic locating of your logo, name, and backlinks that send
readers to your website or another of your distribution
channels. If you have a budget, this might be worth it to you.
Second, if you run your own newsletter, you could partner
by agreeing to exchange professional references, wherein
both parties plug each other's content briefly. Neither
newsletter would actually feature the other person's
content, but you would encourage the reader to visit the

other entity's content. Third, and an evolution of the plug, there could be an exchange of full content. This deal would involve the other newsletter running one of your pieces in full to help drive referral traffic back to your websites, and you do the same thing for them in your newsletter.

My company, Foundation Marketing, and Morning Brew recently used the content-exchange strategy. With six million subscribers, Morning Brew has one of the most popular business newsletters in the world, which made the partnership a wonderful success for us. We ran one of their content pieces in our newsletter, and they did the same for us. Within minutes of the email going out, we had hundreds of new subscribers to Foundation's newsletter, helping grow our brand and distributive reach. Doing this time and time again can unlock hundreds and thousands of new subscribers and reach.

The difficulty rating for newsletter partnerships is a nine out of ten. It's rated so high simply because it takes quite a bit of time and effort to create a win-win relationship with the folks who run the other newsletter.

The Ultimate Benefit: Increased Legitimacy

Partnership distribution can be powerful in widening your audience but also for establishing more legitimacy. If you partner with brands your audience trusts and you're somebody relatively new, associating yourself with that brand can be an amazing way to build credibility and authority. Simply through association, you are gaining credibility as an authority in this space.

Partnerships that are a win-win are something you can always look back on with pride. When I look back to those early days of collaborating with *Social Media Examiner*, I viewed it then as a simple opportunity to increase traffic for my website. What I realize now is that if it wasn't for taking that guest blog post opportunity, I may have never gotten to collaborate with LinkedIn, Hubspot, and so many more. Partnerships have led to a plethora of clients at Foundation Marketing, relationships that have changed the trajectory of my life. The same can be true for you. Partnerships open up an opportunity for engagement, awareness, and a place of authorial breathing room to offer your expertise to the world.

When it comes to partnership distribution, never forget the most important law of partnership physics: find ways to add value to others, and you will get value back.

As your audience grows, understand the community has its own online places where they congregate. They don't only spend time on your content. They have varied communities they go to in order to fully establish their online and human identities. Finding and distributing in those communities gives you an opportunity to keep your audience engaged in material but also grow your reach, a topic which will be explored in the next chapter.

10

COMMUNITY DISTRIBUTION

THE TERMINATOR, PERHAPS THE MOST FAMOUS CINE-matic bot, once said, "I'll be back." In a way, this famous movie line was prophetic. Bots are back and very much in style.

What are bots? For the unfamiliar, bots are autonomous digital programs that interact with systems or users of systems. That's right, real human beings can hold text conversations with an entity that is entirely digital. If that is shocking information to you, you can check the cover of

CREATE ONCE, DISTRIBUTE FOREVER

this book again to make sure you're not reading science fiction. I'll wait.

Are bots interesting? Whether or not you think so personally, hundreds of thousands of Facebook users have joined Groups dedicated to bots and their related technologies. So, I suppose, the answer isn't "yes" or "no" but "there is a very large audience that thinks bots are interesting." These folks love geeking out over the subject, its implications, how to improve bot programming, and how to apply the concept of bots in innovative ways.

This Facebook community forum allows those in the bot orbit to engage in intellectual conversation about scientific progress. It occurs daily. And that's not all. Daily exchange of ideas on artificial intelligence, machine learning, natural language processing, and a whole bunch of other innovative technologies are being discussed in online community settings.

In one of these communities, a member asked the question "What kind of business models are going to come out of the world of bots?" I sensed an opportunity to answer this question with intention and get some ROI from the community. Thankfully, I had already written a blog post that broke down the different business models that could arise from bots. I took that asset and distributed it in this community.

Within minutes, I had five journalists reach out to me. One of those journalists worked for VentureBeat, a site that generates over twenty-six million visits a month. Another journalist happened to own *Chatbots Magazine*, the leading independent online magazine pertaining to bots (yes, this exists). These journalists ran stories about bots business models and referenced my work. Within a matter of days, I was able to reach thousands of additional people, and two of them turned into clients willing to pay more than ten grand per month for marketing services. By creating once and distributing forever, I was able to leverage a community distribution model to expose my expertise and content to vast new audiences.

THE IMPORTANCE OF COMMUNITY DISTRIBUTION

Right now, as you read this, there are millions of people gathering in online communities who are interested in discussing ideas relevant to your content or product. Whether Facebook, Reddit, Slack, Discord, or any other online platform that has community-specific functionality, there are untapped opportunities to reach your target audience.

And I am being serious when I say that *any* topic has a large online following. So rest assured that your target audience can be unlocked through community distribution.

Want some niche examples? The InstantPot Facebook Group has 2.8 million followers. Interested in Dogspotting? So are 1.8 million others on Facebook. There are also communities talking about email automation tools. Others about e-commerce market fit. Literally every single topic you can think of has a community you can join and distribute your topic-relevant stories or products.

The most essential definition of community distribution is identifying online groups of people who gather to discuss topics related to your content brand and then distribute your content or asset into that community for their consumption. The communities can be directly related to your content or product, but they can also be indirectly related. Communities centered around some peripheral idea are still worthwhile. For example, a group about business leadership might have a significant percentage of followers interested in content about accounting, so post your accounting content there (if you have it).

Beyond specific topics, communities can be a gathering place based on an identity that resonates with your content or product. Participation in these communities is defined by who they are as people. Using the hypothetical example of accountants again, this could be an online community where members identify their membership because they are accountants, not just anybody interested in business.

Unlocking the potential of community channels for your distribution strategy is a great way to grow and scale your brand. Throughout this chapter, I will cover some of the major ways in which community channels can be leveraged.

FACEBOOK GROUPS STRATEGIES

There are over ten million Facebook Groups with nearly two billion users in those Groups. Facebook Groups are one of the fastest-growing parts of the platform. The reason is simple: folks can go to a place quickly and conveniently to discuss things they truly care about within a private online community of like-minded people.

Anyone can administer a Facebook Group, which makes it easy to think that these groups are where people go to complain and things won't be moderated. If you are part of your neighborhood Facebook Group, that's especially true. It seems like, in my neighborhood Group, all we do is complain about each other's pets pooping in each other's yards.

In reality, Facebook Groups are an economic juggernaut. It may be surprising to read, but actual business is being done by actual professionals who connect through Facebook Groups every single day.

How to get into these communities to distribute your content and unlock business happens in two straightforward ways: in your own Facebook Groups and in others' Groups.

Strategy 1: Your Own Facebook Groups

- **Goal**: Control the chain of communication with your audience to drive ROI.
- **Difficulty Rating**: 9/10

Create your own Facebook Group by identifying a topic or subject matter that is meaningful to your target audience. It could be as specific or as broad as you want.

In terms of specific Groups, the Group could be focused on your content or product, especially if you have a pre-established audience due to other distribution channels. Or, if you are still growing your customer base, include a call-to-action on your website for users and visitors to join your company Group. You can promote that call to action when people make a purchase, consume a piece of content, or sign up for your newsletter.

As you accumulate more members for this Group, you now have access to a large pool of people.

Jasper, which provides AI copywriting, leveraged their own Facebook Group with wild success. They accumulated

followers and Group members in order to generate awareness about their brand and product features. There are
currently over 67,000 members of Jasper's AI copywriting Group. Presumably, these folks are mostly made up of
professionals in the field, such as marketers, copywriters,
business leaders, and others interested in their services.
Every time Jasper creates a new feature, a new product, or
has worthwhile information about the company to share,
they're able to reach their community instantly. Because of
this Group's reach and other market factors, Jasper raised
$125 million and had a $1.5 billion valuation in 2022.

But the world of SaaS and B2B marketing isn't the only
surprising space using Facebook Groups. All kinds of niche
products, services, and content types can thrive there.
Consider Roo & You, a wonderfully eclectic furniture company that sells malleable couches and seats intended for
children but can be used by the entire family. A Roo & You
couch can be bent, folded, and manipulated into various
fort-like configurations. Essentially, the furniture allows
the customer to make and play on forts with one's kids.

I am a member of the Roo & You Facebook Group. My
family and I were highly anticipating the release of a
specific product we knew was on the horizon, thanks to
a Group update. When that product was finally released,
we and around 19,000 other people went in and made the

purchase within a day. Imagine running a company where one distribution channel meant you could sell 19,000 units of your product in a day. That's a fantastic return on distribution investment!

So, how can you grow the size of your own Group? Beyond adding a call-to-action on your various channels, post your content into this group just like you would any other distribution channel. Follow the execution guidance, such as following the Four *E*'s and Facebook's conventions, detailed in Chapter 8.

Strategy 2: Joining or Buying
Other People's Facebook Groups

- **Goal**: Build authority amongst your target and drive new traffic.
- **Difficulty Rating**: 7/10

You don't always have to reinvent the wheel and start from scratch. There are already Facebook Groups out there with sizable audiences. Go to the Facebook search bar and look for these communities.

Use relevant keywords that reflect your ideal audience and find the communities they belong to. Join these Groups! Once you've been added by the Group admin, it's imperative you read the rules of engagement. Are you allowed to share links? Are you allowed to be self-promotional? Are you allowed to share your own content? Is it a read-only community, or can you engage with posts and post items?

With the rules understood, it's time to start acting on them. Ideally, you want to be able to comment and post in these groups so that you may begin your distribution strategies. Look or wait for posts about content you've already created or covered elsewhere. Create once, distribute forever, after all. Reply to that thread by seeding your content and letting folks know there is a solution to their question or further information to consider.

If only admins are allowed to post, reach out to them to see if they believe your content is worth sharing with the Group. Another reason to reach out to the administrator is if you have a budget. You can sponsor Groups and pay money for your content to be posted, or, maybe your sponsorship somehow alters the Group's banner or logo to reflect your brand.

Here's an example of a successful reachout to a Group administrator. When I was hiring an executive assistant, I went looking at all of the various Facebook Groups about executive assistants. None would admit me as a member. So, I reached out to the administrators of a few of these Groups, paid them fifty dollars, and they posted the job application. Within a matter of minutes, I had a flood of applicants reaching out who were exceedingly qualified to do the work.

As you review Groups, you may notice that some of them haven't been updated in a while but still maintain large membership. Like some Pages, these might be graveyard Groups. If you can afford to do so, consider inquiring about the purchase of these Groups from the administrator. It could be an excellent way to jumpstart your Group audience. You can then distribute your content or product with them and unlock amazing returns relative to the investment.

Facebook Follies

Facebook Groups can be a tough community distribution channel to use, especially if you are running your own Group. Running your own Facebook group receives a difficulty rating of nine out of ten, and it needs to be acknowledged that running your own Group is more difficult than using other people's Groups. Therefore, other people's Facebook groups will receive a rating of seven out of ten.

Nurturing and consistently growing your own community can be extremely time-consuming and requires constant curation from you. In the early stages, if you're starting from scratch, you will be putting in a lot more work than the revenue likely returned. If your Group begins to scale and grow bigger, the amount of labor involved then becomes too vast for the founder or first marketing hire. That means you'll need to be prepared to hire a community manager and have the capacity to incur that cost.

Other people's Facebook Groups are easier to unlock because there is no start-from-zero situation. The community is already there, engaged, and ready to consume. Your hurdles involve getting access to the Group, playing by the Group rules, possibly coordinating sponsorship opportunities, or outright buying the Group.

SUBREDDIT STRATEGIES

- **Goal**: Drive referral traffic from Reddit to your content or website.
- **Difficulty Rating**: 10/10

Despite Reddit's massive volume of users, marketers tend to break out into hives every time they think about distributing there. That's probably for good reason. Reddit will ban you very, very quickly if they think you are overtly marketing on their channel. Reddit and redditors hate marketing.

Have I imbued you with enough confidence yet? Oh, I haven't? Well, consider this. Redditors don't like marketers because they don't like being marketed to. Another way to put it: Redditors want to consume useful content, find stories, and get specific information they're looking for. Therefore, you need to adopt a distribution strategy that adheres to the channel's rules and perspectives, a kind of anti-marketing marketing, if you will. If content comes first in Reddit communities, you need to lead with authentic content.

Links and Subreddits

A subreddit is a community devoted to a specific conversation, question, or subject. Like other massive online communities, many subreddits have follower numbers in the millions. The subreddit "r/science," also known as Reddit Science or The New Reddit Journal of Science, has twenty-eight million members. The takeaway here is that there are millions of folks in your target audience waiting for your content in this online space. There are a lot of opportunities to drive referral traffic from subreddits to your website or product. My hope is that your referral clicks come in at such break-neck speeds that you crash Reddit's website. (Just kidding, Reddit administrators, if you're reading this.)

Redditors love links. We did our own analysis, and while text posts seem to provide redditors with valuable information, the content that generated the most upvotes were those that were links. Here is a chart of the study:

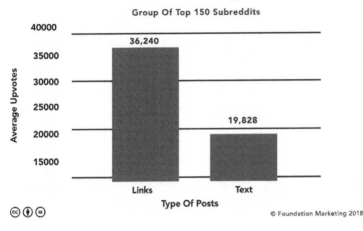

Figure 10.1

Before you start submitting a bunch of links to random subreddits, do a bit of research into the subreddits you plan to share your content in. Here's how to do it: Look through subreddits on your own to make a determination as to which subreddits align with your content. Using Reddit's search bar, choose keywords relevant to your audience to navigate more quickly to subreddits that could speak to them. Look through the posts to see if they resemble content or ideas consistent with your content or product's mission.

Content-Market Fit on Reddit

When you identify a subreddit as being ideal for your audience, you don't want to just guess and assume the content you provide is going to be something they want. I made this mistake in r/technology, and I thought my blog posts about software-as-a-service would fly. Well, I was immediately banned, as you know. Because I didn't carefully find authentic ways to seed specific blogs into specific places, I was flagged as self-promotional. The lesson I learned was that content fit for subreddits has to be perfectly aligned in order to be considered genuine.

Not only do you need to be extremely careful about how you post your content on a subreddit, you also need to understand that different subreddit communities have different content expectations. That means you need to study the most popular posts in a given subreddit. The good news is that it's easy to sort the posts based on the most upvotes, shares, and comments. Isolate these popular posts and, putting on the Sherlock Homeboy hat, study what makes them unique, reverse-engineer those features, and then use them to inform the posting of your own content.

A Closely-Moderated Community

Redditors and Reddit moderators are some of the savviest people on the internet. They can see through anything.

That means the difficulty rating for successfully seeding content onto Reddit is ten out of ten. If you go into this community distribution channel thinking like a promoter, you will be banned.

Redditors only engage with people who have good intentions. So, ensure your seeding and posting to this online community is genuine, not overtly self-promotional, pertains to a conversation happening in the subreddit, and adds value.

One of the biggest tips I can offer you is to lean heavily into flattery, celebration, and the empowerment of other users. That has helped me get on the front page of Reddit several times. Instead of just acting like a rogue marketer lurking in the shadows and posting content based on analytics, it will benefit your success if you also engage with the community and show your appreciation.

SLACK STRATEGIES

- **Goal**: Reach your audience and drive referral traffic from Slack to your content or website.
- **Difficulty Rating**: 6/10

I know what a lot of you are thinking. "Isn't Slack an internal business communication tool meant for colleagues and teams?" Well, yes and no. It's actually a lot more versatile than that. At its core, Slack is a community distribution channel where anyone can go to talk about topics that concern them.

It's a channel where people talk about finances, make plans for the weekend, host video calls, or share voice notes. It's not necessarily a well-known distribution channel where brands and businesses think there are untapped audiences. But it turns out that Slack communities are growing. For example, there are Slack communities dedicated to health professionals. Doctors all over the world join these channels (Slack calls its individual communities "channels") to talk about their profession, career pathways, changes on the horizon for medicine, and other topics that might concern them. Whether doctors or another occupation, it's a place where like-minded folks connect but also solve problems.

In some ways, Slack is like a combination of Facebook Groups and subreddits. Slack channels tend to be exclusionary, tight-knit, and focused on relatively specific professions or subjects like Facebook. But they are also moderated carefully like Reddit. You do have to be careful. If they notice somebody coming into a channel with no clear professional alignment and spamming their content, that distributor will get banned.

If you can identify Slack communities where your target audience spends their time and enter them with good intentions, you have an opportunity to distribute your content to those channels and direct referral traffic back to your content.

Studying Community Structure

The first step for leveraging Slack channels as community distribution channels involves joining and studying any given community. How often do people interact? How many links are shared on a regular basis? Sometimes topics have dedicated "links" channels, spaces where frequently sharing links is acceptable. To what degree is the channel directly or indirectly about the content you create? Answering these kinds of questions will help guide your choices about how to carefully seed your content.

You'll need to keep note of which channels you can freely share links in and which you can't. As you become a frequent collaborator and contributor to these channels, you'll connect with other people, which will often include connecting with the channel administrator. Like with other channels, you might consider sponsoring your content on a Slack channel.

When It Comes to Promotion, Slack Doesn't Lack

Slack's culture is one that makes it an easier channel to distribute on, and I give it a difficulty rating of six out of ten. Unlike Reddit, Slack is a community channel that, to a degree, encourages users to share their ideas via content and links. When your authentic posts start adding value, members cheer you on to share your stuff.

There is a culture within Slack that is much more goal-oriented or collaboratively answer-seeking than other channels. Compared to other, more restrictive channels, Slack is an open place willing to give people a chance.

DISCORD STRATEGIES

- **Goal**: Distribute your content on a channel other than your website.
- **Difficulty Rating**: 8/10

Discord is a chatroom-based platform. One of the biggest barriers keeping content distributors away from Discord is their belief that it's a channel extensively used for gaming. While that may have been true at some point in Discord's past, the channel has become a much broader chat platform to discuss anything.

It has traditional, text-based, and modern video-based chat rooms. Video chats allow screen-sharing and presentational tools to tailor an experience, not unlike Zoom.

Discord's branding refers to these chatroom communities as "Servers." And now that a generation has grown up familiar with its interface and usefulness, more and more companies are starting to launch their own Discord Servers to capture their audience's attention and distribute their content. As time goes on, it stands to reason that Discord will become a channel that is more and more native to *any* target audience. If your audience uses Discord, you can create your own Server that speaks to their interests and aligns with your content or product.

Conversation Overload

Because this platform is chatroom-based, it takes quite a bit of work. Conversations can happen quickly and constantly, making it nearly impossible to track the relevant-to-you messages. Conversation overload might burn you out of your ability to distribute your content elsewhere.

For these reasons, and if you have the resources, consider staying active in this community by placing somebody on your team into a distribution management role inside of Discord. Not only will your content be distributed to new audiences, doing so will increase your organization's understanding of how to implement best practices inside of specific Discord communities.

Furthermore, organizing your brand or company's content into several different Servers is a great way to help your Discord community and followers understand the way you shape Discord content for their needs. For example, organizations like Hypebeast, a men's fashion brand, developed several Discord Servers tailored toward specific client needs and wants. There is a Server devoted to their Discord community rules, and another devoted to announcements, another devoted to the launch of new shoe products. You get the idea. They get specific. And they even provide links to their own content channels for followers to find out more.

By listing both their Discord Servers and their other channels, Discord can act as a distribution channel for other distribution channels. Very meta. The Discord audience is incentivized to check out Hypebeast's content on YouTube, Instagram, Twitter, TikTok, Facebook, and Pinterest. That's free distribution working for them.

Hypebeast has 31,000 people connected to their Discord. That means every time they post a launch schedule, it caters directly to the folks interested in buying their products.

The benefit of Discord's in-app versatility as well as its connection to all other channels means it increases the likelihood of driving traffic, sales, and business back to your website.

I can vouch for the power of Discord with confidence because one of my clients at Foundation Marketing—a client in the world of Web3—wanted to grow their audience through content marketing. My company decided the best market-fit was with Discord, which somewhat surprised the client because it wasn't on their radar. Once we created and distributed the content in a carefully chosen Discord channel, it quickly blew up. For context, this company had around 37,000 followers across its channels but saw 650,000 total engagements after seeding to Discord. It was the best-performing piece of content the client ever had.

Discord's End Game

At the time of writing, Discord does still skew heavily toward the gaming community. Perhaps because of that reason, it's a community distribution channel that is still relatively new to most professional marketers. That can create a steep learning curve. Therefore, I place Discord's difficulty rating at an eight out of ten.

Because the audience is waiting in the wings to grow from gamers to professionals, the number of opportunities is still limited. There are not as many active use cases in the business world like other community-driven channels, but that they are growing in Discord suggests its status as a rocket channel.

USERS ARE SAVVY

Now that we've covered some major community distribution channels, remember that a strong distribution strategy means going to the communities in which your audience spends time. It's up to you to embrace the idea of studying your audience, knowing where they're spending their time, and then going into those communities to distribute your stories. Users are savvy at finding the communities that speak to their needs, and you need to be savvy at finding their communities, too.

Have empathy and understand how both the community and individuals conduct themselves. Any distribution you seed needs to add value to their lives and their immediate pain points. It needs to resonate with them. Your material should feel collaborative and authentic. If you are able to take off your marketing hat and lead with human dignity, you can unlock the opportunities that community channels provide, which are substantial.

But, community distribution is not the biggest opportunity. The greatest distribution opportunity of our generation is *search* distribution. More people use search engines as a channel for gathering information than any other method. How will you leverage that traffic? Search distribution will be reviewed in the next chapter.

SEARCH DISTRIBUTION

BILLIONS OF ONLINE SEARCHES HAPPEN EVERY DAY. Guide those searching back to your content.

Many years ago, I wrote a search-optimized blog post called "26 Hustle Quotes to Get You Motivated and Inspired." It mixes my own quotations with those of successful business people like Steve Jobs, Mark Cuban, and Richard Branson. These inspirational quotes have been read by millions of people because, all around the world, people look for quotes to get inspired.

I published this list of quotes on my own website, and today it has over 600 comments. It generates thousands of visits every day, and I've seen tons of influencers rely on this post when coming up with their own social posts. After realizing how much traction this piece was getting, I decided that I needed to make it work harder for me. I took the time to update this blog post with entrepreneurship and hustle-related quotes from yours truly. Fast forward a few weeks and I was constantly being tagged on Instagram, Twitter, LinkedIn, and Facebook by someone sharing one of my quotes.

Putting on my Sherlock Homeboy hate, the mystery of this post's impact simply led to the question "Why?" Why does this specific piece generate so much engagement for me and rank so well for multiple years? Quite simply, it was optimized for search. When anybody goes to Google and they type in "hustle quote," my piece of content shows up and people get exactly what they want. It appears on Google's first page of search results, and it's likely in the top five if you do that search today.

And why does this distribution channel have a chance to work so well for you too? The 40,000 users who search Google every second. Yes, that's how many folks you can reach by the time you're done reading this sentence. Google processes over one-and-a-quarter *trillion* searches annually for billions of users. These numbers are mind-boggling. Even if you capture a tiny fraction of a percent of these users, distribution through search can create life-changing revenue.

If you are creating content, ranking in Google is arguably the most powerful way to distribute your content. Most search experiences start with Google. And many multi-million-dollar companies over the years have been built on the back of Google by optimizing themselves for search distribution. It's allowed organizations to unlock millions and billions of dollars worth of value and market cap. Now I want to help you do the same.

When it comes to search distribution, there are two central forms: SEO and paid distribution. Let's look at both.

SEO DISTRIBUTION STRATEGIES

- **Goal**: Capture organic traffic from sites like Google.
- **Difficulty Rating**: 8/10

Search engine optimization (SEO) is the act of producing or editing content in such a way that it ranks after a user inputs a search engine inquiry. If you can uncover the different, common ways your target audience goes to Google (or other search engines) to search to solve their problems, you can unlock an amazing distribution channel. It involves optimizing the content on your website and other published content to ensure that when certain keywords are typed into a search engine, your content will appear on the first page of the search results.

A lot of marketers have oversold the complexity of what needs to be done for a great search distribution strategy. I believe it's a very simple, three-stage process:

1. First, understand the people that you're trying to connect with and the things that they type into Google.

2. Second, the best search engine distribution returns come from aligning your content with intent. I'm convinced the most underrated part of search distribution strategy is the ability to root recommendations in search intent. In other words, make sure your website and content are able to be found by Google's algorithm.

3. And third, when people arrive and view your content, make sure it's actually of high value.

Ensuring these three elements—understanding search intent, encouraging your website's discovery by the search engine, and creating high-value content—will create the circumstances for a successful search distribution game plan.

Let's break down all three in a little bit more detail.

Strategy 1: Search Intent

The term "search intent" describes how your target audience uses search engines. Search intent should be studied in universities, because too few understand the role search plays in buying decisions. Smart brands study the intent behind a keyword just as much as they study the volume associated with it. Analytics show that how a user structures their search is indicative of their motivations or endgame hopes for the search, whether that's researching, looking for a specific product or service, or getting ready for purchase.

Overall, there are four types of search intent:

1. Informational, or searches looking for information or answers.
2. Commercial investigation, or searches exploring purchase options.
3. Navigational, or searches directly to a known solution.
4. Transactional, or searches on how to facilitate a desired purchase.

Here is a breakdown of keywords and how they indicate a user's desired behavior.

SEARCH INTENT			
Informational	**Commercial Investigation**	**Navigational**	**Transactional**
What	Best	Brand Name	Price
Who	Top	Product Name	Buy
Why	Review	Service Name	Coupon
Where	Color		Cheap
How	Comparison		Discount
Guides	Size		Pricing
Templates			
Ideas			
Examples			
Learn			
Tutorial			

Figure 11.1

Each list of words demonstrates like-minded search inquiries. Each search-intent category represents a different motivation or desired solution to the user's pain point. Understanding our users' pain points is part and parcel of creating SEO-winning content, so let's look at each category in a little more detail.

INFORMATIONAL

Thankfully, the terms themselves are somewhat self-explanatory. Informational searches are when users are looking for, well, information. There isn't any intent to buy a product at this stage. Perhaps they are on the buyer's journey, but a purchase is far away. Even so, it is valuable to your brand to get their eyes on your content to keep you in their mind as they progress toward purchase.

These searches are typified by the who, what, when, why, and how questions. "What goes well with barbecue?" "Who was the first president?" "Why is the sky blue?" "Where is the nearest Home Depot?" These are informational queries, but we can tell that a few of them seem to have purchases in their future. Somebody may be buying food to bring to the barbecue while another might need to buy some tools or materials for a house project. So, even though there is an educational intent, informational searches have value.

COMMERCIAL INVESTIGATIONS

The next form of intent, commercial investigations are searches that demonstrate the user is interested in making a commercial purchase but first wants to conduct some research to inform their purchasing decisions. They include adjective-focused language to help refine their results.

"The *best* pillows for a sore back."

"The *top* coffee machines of 2035."

"Compact blue blenders."

We can see these users are another step farther along in the buyer's journey. They are not so much looking for basic information as they are purchase-specific information. Their desire is to generate an awareness of what's available to them and what they might want, not unlike looking over options at a grocery store and scanning the food label for further information like ingredients, expiration date, and so on. Commercial investigation searches will be driven by features that appeal most to the consumer.

NAVIGATIONAL

Navigation searches are even farther down the buyer's journey. At this point, the user is actually typing in your brand, website, or business name. Perhaps they know they already want to make a purchase or want to peruse your website for more information before they make a purchase. Either way, they know what they want and they just want to get there.

TRANSACTIONAL

Transactional searches are the equivalent of placing the groceries on the conveyor belt at the checkout line. It'll be moments before the *cha-ching* of the cash register, and the purchase is on the horizon.

There may be some semblance of a user still shopping, but they are in the home stretch of the buyer's journey. They know what they need, and they type in words like "price" or "discount" to see if they can find the product for a better price when comparing major e-commerce stores.

THE SEARCHERS

Once you understand the psychological intent around why people are going to Google and typing in the things they search for, you can create content to answer your target audience's most common needs and questions. That means dropping these searched phrases into your content across the board to generate more engagement from the Google algorithm. What those phrases are will depend on your content, service, or product, and hopefully, you are running analytics to make those discoveries.

So, what does your target audience search for most? And how do they search for it?

Somebody searching Google for "best CRM" (commercial investigation) compared to another user typing in "What's CRM?" (informational) is looking for different things. The first person is likely scouring for recommendations for the most useful CRM products available on the market. The search engine results will reflect that by prioritizing review sites, blog posts, YouTube reviewers, two

CREATE ONCE, DISTRIBUTE FOREVER

or three landing pages, and four to five advertisements for products. The results themselves will be designed to help the searcher identify and act on acquiring the best CRM.

The searcher who typed "What is CRM?" will see a completely different set of content on the search-results page. Ranking links would be informational sites like Wikipedia. But that doesn't mean this searcher will avoid marketing. They will likely encounter brands that have embraced a search engine optimization strategy.

What most people don't realize is that brands are spending thousands of dollars right now to rank in search. But why pay to rank when you can optimize keywords with your new knowledge? Optimizing content is an inexpensive way to distribute. For example, it's estimated that there are 95,000 searches a month for "What is CRM?" It just so happens that a 2016 Salesforce post ranks for it every single year because they optimize it annually (rather than pay). They treat optimization like an investment.

When you can isolate the searches your audience uses, it presents you the opportunity to deliver highly valuable assets to the searcher that also directly answer their search engine inputs or questions. The user's ranking keywords might be at different stages of the buyer's journey, but they're still valuable. That is the heart of search distribution: you create content that satisfies the search intent. The more clicks and links your content receives, the more Google will be pleased to send searchers to your work.

Strategy 2: Getting Discovered by Google

Making sure that your website can be found by Google is a pretty open-and-shut situation. If your website is built with HTML with no weird code and iframes, flash, or other outdated techniques, it's likely going to be easily findable for search engines. I don't expect you to be a coder, and you may have to work with an engineer to accomplish some of these things. Nonetheless, here are some ways to optimize your website for SEO distribution.

You will need tags. What are tags? They are bits of coding meant for search engines to analyze the content of your website(s). Search engines have a technology called a "crawler," which examines your tags in order to glean whether or not your content fits well with a search inquiry. The next obvious step is optimizing your tags for SEO. How do you do that? There are a number of ways.

TITLE TAGS

Results are primarily driven by title tags. Best practice is to use the same title of your piece of content in the code itself to avoid confusion. You don't want a user to input a commercial investigation inquiry only to land on your information page because you offered a misleading title tag.

How would this look in the code? Well, for my hustle quotes article, it would look like this: "<title>26 Hustle Quotes to Get You Motivated and Inspired<title>". That's a bit technical, and it's outside the scope of this book to explain how HTML works precisely, but what you need to know is by inserting that title tag in to the HTML, the search engine will prioritize this article for any inquiry with the words "hustle" or "quote" right next to each other. It will hit "motivated" and "inspired" searches, too. But, it will hit "hustle quote" more efficiently than "motivational quotes" because of the way the title is written. So, my content's title and the title tag have been optimized for an audience that searches for "hustle quotes" specifically.

META DESCRIPTION TAGS

Meta description tags also have a powerful influence on optimized results. They are the second-most important HTML feature to use for SEO.

What are they? Go to Google right now and do any kind of search. You were bound to do one today, so now's the time. As you scroll through the results, you might notice that there are links just below where the webpage preview stops. These links can be of all sorts, but the two you'll consistently see as first and second are "Meta Title" (the title tag) and "Meta Description" (the meta description tag).

Meta description tags are longer, like a phrase or complete sentence, and capture the keywords or possible search inquiries of the content. The coding works similarly to title tags, and the crawler will identify relevance based on the language of the meta description tag.

ALT IMAGE TAGS

In other areas of the book, I've illustrated how using images for various channels is crucial for their respective distribution strategy. I've even used my own illustrative images to help guide you. Why? Images themselves add variance to text-based information and engage readers. Presumably, you are using images in many of your pieces of content. Let them do extra SEO work for you by giving them ALT image tags.

Using the HTML, give your images a one- or two-word tag that Google can use when optimizing a search for a user. Going back to my hustle quotes article, I already expressed how it would rank more efficiently if the search inquiry was "hustle quotes" instead of "motivational quotes." If I wanted to get closer to ranking when the word "motivational" is used, I might add "motivational" as one of my ALT image tags.

LINKS

Your content's SEO can be optimized with links in two ways:

1. The high-quality links included in your own content, *or*
2. If other high-quality websites have links to your content.

Google and other search engines scan that linked data in their determination as to whether or not your content is relevant to a given search. The stronger the SEO of those links (and the more it does), the more relevant your article becomes for SEO.

The golden rule is to never link to content that is unrelated or spammy. The words in your linked content should match the context of the linked content. To Google, that communicates what and why an article will have much more relevance for the user upon clicking the link.

Further, you should also consider mixing and matching the types of links you build from the outside pointing in. Generally, there are backlinks and internal links. Backlinks are links to your content that exist on other web pages.

They are an indicator of popularity, authority, and credibility; presumably, websites will link back to you if they find your content valuable or worth reading. And if others find you valuable, Google does, too. Internal links are links within your content that go to other content on your website. But again, quality over quantity. High-quality internal links that align with your tags are best.

Strategy 3: High-Value Content

To complete the SEO recipe, the content on your website needs to be of high value. What does it mean for content to be "high value," though? Content is not valuable in a vacuum. Rather, its value is determined by the reader and whether or not the content is actually helpful for satisfying the intent behind their search.

Google rewards content they believe will offer high value to the user looking for a keyword or phrase. If the content you create is not satisfying to the user's intent—in the sense that the content does not actually give them the answers to their questions, suggestions, or directive in achieving the goals of their search—Google is less likely to show your content in the search engine results page.

Your content becomes high-value by better understanding the problems and pain points by going in as much depth as possible. When you do this, two things happen. First, you generate retention. Users start to read your content and stay there. Second, two other people will link to your content from around the internet. When that happens, Google is tracking these behaviors, both links and traffic. As they increase, Google will increasingly suggest your content in its results page. By actually solving the user's problem, you are increasing the likelihood of ranking in Google and tapping into this distribution strategy.

Getting Lost in the Frey

SEO distribution is a channel that can be harnessed by almost anyone but can take a lot of work as you increase competition. The difficulty rating is an eight out of ten. Its difficulty will always be exacerbated by specific market niches that apply to you. If you are starting from scratch, you will have a more difficult time seeding backlinks to improve your SEO. If your content happens to be in a flooded or in-demand industry with tons of competitors, you will be up against three competitive factors:

1. Other brands are likely paying for their content to rank, and
2. Your credibility still needs to improve
3. Your site doesn't have as many pages that rank yet

With that said, paying for your distribution is the other major form of search distribution. Obviously, creating something for free using SEO tactics helps the bottom line, but when you clock the hours it takes relative to how much you might pay to rank, paid media distribution might be the way to go.

PAID SEARCH DISTRIBUTION STRATEGIES

- **Goal**: Capture paid traffic from relevant websites, newsletters, podcasts, or other online channels.
- **Difficulty Rating**: 3/10

Google and other search engines make the vast majority of their money from paid advertising. Yes, Google directs the bulk of its users to paid advertising—called "native ads" meant to feel like natural search results. Google is not the organic-traffic giant that many perceive them to be.

The caveat that we need to address early is, of course, if you can't afford paid search distribution, then you probably will want to focus on and leverage SEO distribution or other organic techniques in this book. But, if you do have a budget, you should consider how paid search distribution can play a role in your overall strategy and skyrocket you to the top of the SERP (search engine results page).

Paid search distribution a.k.a. Search Engine Marketing (SEM) is the act of buying advertising space on the search engine results page that shows up before the organic results. Being the very first or second (depending on competitors buying space) item seen by the searcher has profound effects on clicks and traffic. In short, you will capture a lot more traffic the higher you rank. More traffic leads to more sales or revenue for you.

As you are strategizing and budgeting, it's good to have a general understanding of the payment structure. There are two to four ads at the top of a given Google search. Those placements come with different costs, the top slot being the top cost. The companies who bid for those spots will be charged per user click, which is called a cost per click (CPC). (Not a pro tip but a fun tip: clicking on the ads of your competitors over and over again charges them money. Don't tell them I sent you.)

There's an easy way to determine if the CPC for a given ad is worth it to you. Calculate and compare your cost per user (CPU) and cost per visitor (CPV). If your spending on advertising and acquiring visits (CPV) is a manageable line item in your CPU budget, then you are good to go. If the CPV is driving up your CPU costs dramatically, you may be spending too much on advertising.

Pocket Money

If you have the budget, running Google ads doesn't take much heavy lifting. Spending money is easy. The difficulty rating for paid media distribution is a three out of ten. The only reason it's not a zero out of ten is because you will have to budget out your expenses to see what you can spend. Coupled with that, you will have to have some understanding of search intent to ensure your ad aligns with your target audience and won't confuse them. If it's not aligned, your brand or content will be marked as unuseful in the user's eyes. But, theoretically, you can spend as much as you want to thank number one.

SEARCHING FOR SUCCESS

Search distribution provides organizations the ability to scale and reach thousands of people every hour. This is because search as a distribution channel is arguably undefeated. When you look at companies like NerdWallet, Canva, Salesforce, Hubspot, Casper, other direct-to-consumer products, and so many others, their success is largely built through search distribution. If they did not come up on the results page when users were searching for answers, their business would be buried.

There is unquestionable value in optimizing your search distribution. It could literally bring millions of people to your content or product. Further, if you consistently update your strategy, you could sustain the life of a piece of content for a long time to come. Search results and the subsequent clicks perpetuate the relevance of your content. It simply makes sense to get the snowball rolling that will accumulate into an avalanche of traffic. But, with great power comes great responsibility. As your content starts to rank, it will influence millions of people for years to come.

I hope the channels and principles that I've shared throughout Part 3 give you a glimpse into your strategic possibility as well as the potential success sitting right in front of you.

At this point, if you've read this thing from top to bottom, you have one of two mindsets. Either you are ready to go and start distributing your content or you want a little guidance on how to take the first steps. If the latter, it's your lucky day. In the next and final chapter, I'm going to deliver a playbook. It will outline how to take all of the principles you've studied—the ideas and the techniques—and clearly break them down into checklists, an example weekly schedule, and a three-step beginner's guide.

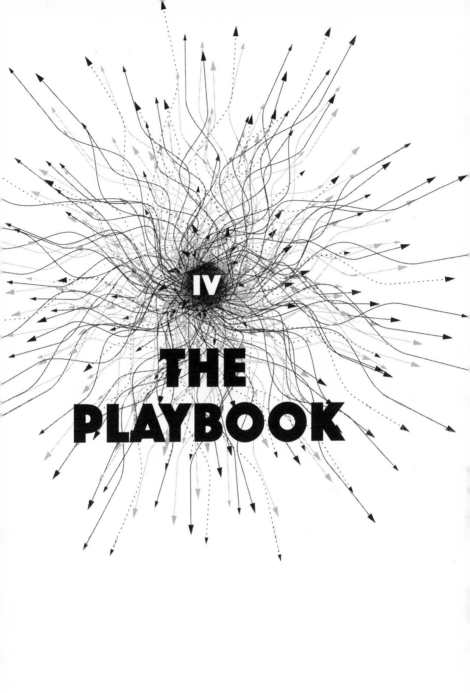

IV

THE
PLAYBOOK

12

THE CONTENT DISTRIBUTION PLAYBOOK

W E'VE TALKED A LOT ABOUT DISTRIBUTION, including different channels, the importance of remixing and republishing, and the transformative opportunities distribution provides. Hidden beneath all of the concepts and techniques is the idea that a hands-off strategy—otherwise known as chance—is never successful. You have to hustle and work to make distribution work for you. It's not going to happen overnight.

What I want to do now is give you a very simple play-book to get the ball rolling. The templates and steps discussed throughout can be used by you or your team to ensure that every single piece of content you create can be distributed forever.

By having this playbook—something you can use over and over again—you will increase the likelihood that you implement successful distribution strategies. When you look at the playbook I offer here, it's not exclusively going to fit your situation. You will need to embrace the Sherlock Homeboy Method by reverse-engineering the elements of this playbook that will be most useful for you. Customize your playbook, just like a football team might, in order to find the right strategy and beat the competition.

Let's get started.

PLAY 1: CONTENT DISTRIBUTION CHECKLIST

It's great to feel inspired and to learn from reading, but it's execution time. Checklists can be an essential tool for guaranteeing success in almost any life accomplishment. For example, when I moved out of my first apartment, I wanted to make sure I got as much of my deposit back as possible. So I went online and snagged a cleaning checklist to ensure I didn't miss anything. It had things like:

- "Sweep the floors."
- "Wipe the baseboards."
- "Clean the doors."
- "Empty the refrigerator."
- "Cycle the dishwasher."
- "Dust the blinds."

The whole nine yards. Some of it was relevant. Some of it was irrelevant. All of it was a guided reminder, and I could identify the items to check off based on my situation, in order to maximize the return of my deposit.

One-size-fits-all is not something that applies to checklists. But when a checklist has *everything* you could possibly need, it's a worthwhile document to help pick and choose what will lead to your specific definition of success. That type of checklist is what you have here.

Content Distribution Checklist

Content marketers: You don't win by pressing publish.

You win by distributing it. You win with shares. You win by earning links. You win by being featured in newsletters. You win when a prospect shares it with their boss. You win with more leads. **You win by driving action**. The checklist below highlights more than one hundred different ways to distribute your content after pressing publish.

Want to put your distribution skills to the test and learn our exact two-week content distribution process? We've created a twelve-day **Distribution Challenge** that'd be perfect for you. *Join the distribution challenge today.*

#	Tactic	☑
FACEBOOK DISTRIBUTION		
1	Share the content on your company Facebook page.	☐
2	Share the content on your personal account. Set privacy to public.	☐
3	Use Facebook advertising to distribute the content to a broader audience than your page would likely reach.	☐
4	Join Facebook groups and share the content you've developed in them as soon as it's published.	☐
5	Comment in Facebook groups when people ask questions about similar topics. Add value before the link.	☐
6	Use retargeting display or Facebook ads to connect with your mailing list. Upload your list and you can target these individuals.	☐
7	Reach out to a few of your closest friends on Facebook and ask them if they'd mind sharing the content.	☐
8	Create a Note or Instant Article on Facebook that drives to the content you've developed or is a repurposed version of the content.	☐
9	Pin the content to the top of your Facebook page.	☐
10	Share and @Mention any brands referenced in the piece.	☐

11	Share a graphic with a CTA in your Facebook story.	☐
12	Run remarketing ads against people who have visited your site lately.	☐
13	Run remarketing ads against people who have watched 20+ seconds of your video.	☐
14	Run a news feed ad promoting the post.	☐

TWITTER DISTRIBUTION

15	Share your content on Twitter so your followers are aware of it.	☐
16	Share the key points as a micro-blog on Twitter and link to the piece.	☐
17	Retweet posts from users who are sharing your content on their own Twitter accounts.	☐
18	Respond to people who are sharing other pieces of content you have created.	☐
19	Bump your tweets by replying to the initial tweet.	☐
20	Create a tweet storm about the problem your article solves. Link to the article at the end.	☐
21	Share links of this asset on other channels. Ex. Link to the repurposed LinkedIn post, Growth Hackers post, Hacker News, etc.	☐
22	Mention the influencers who you included in the content on Twitter. RT-bait.	☐
23	Create imagery with quotes from people in the content and tag on Twitter. RT-bait.	☐

24   Send direct messages to a few of your followers
      letting them know you just wrote a post they might be   ☐
      interested in. Include a link to the tweet.

25   Offer to take part in a Twitter chat and reference your   ☐
      content throughout.

26   Pin the content to the top of your Twitter account.   ☐

LINKEDIN DISTRIBUTION

27   Share a status update about the content. Tag the
      influencers who you mentioned in the content within
      your status update or spread it out over the week so   ☐
      there are multiple posts.

28   Write a blog post on LinkedIn that drives readers
      back to your content. It will give a notification to the
      majority of your connections so they see the activity   ☐
      surrounding the post.

29   Share your content within niche communities and
      groups on LinkedIn that are relevant to your content.   ☐
      Jason Quey wrote a great post on this tactic.

30   Export the emails of your contacts on LinkedIn and   ☐
      reach out to them.

31   Export the emails of your contacts on LinkedIn and run
      ads using Facebook custom audiences that tell them to   ☐
      check out your latest piece of content.

32   Run advertising on LinkedIn from your company page   ☐
      driving users to click and read your content.

33   Share images that come directly from the asset and link   ☐
      to it as a post.

34	Share the SlideShare deck via "Files" on LinkedIn.	☐
35	Create a video announcing the launch of this new asset. Share a link.	☐
36	Drive people to content with "sponsored InMail."	☐
37	Create a long-form status update about the article with a link in the comments.	☐
38	Comment on status updates shared on LinkedIn with a link to the asset.	☐

SNAPCHAT DISTRIBUTION

39	Share a QR code that is connected to your content.	☐
40	Send a snap directly to your connections telling them to check out your latest.	☐
41	Share a video to your story telling people what your content is about and tell them how to find it.	☐
42	Create a Snapstorm (multiple snaps one after another) that talks about a portion of your content and tell viewers to click the link.	☐
43	Send one-to-one Snapchat DMs asking people to check out your latest.	☐
44	Send one-to-one Snapchat DMs asking people to give you an upvote on one of the various sites you submitted your content to.	☐
45	Share a URL in your story and tell your followers to screenshot the snap to get it on their camera roll.	☐
46	Run a Snapchat ad targeting individuals in a specific region.	☐

INSTAGRAM DISTRIBUTION

47	Share a post on Instagram that tells your followers to click the link in your bio, which happens to be a link to your content.	☐
48	Run paid advertising on Instagram driving users to see your content.	☐
49	Share on your story with a swipe-up link.	☐
50	Pay influencers to share a link and swipe-up CTA on their story.	☐
51	Find people that are using hashtags that are relevant to you and comment on their content.	☐
52	Pay influencers to share a visual on their feed and change their link in the bio to your post.	☐
53	Send a DM to followers who have recently engaged with your content.	☐
54	Share the feed post on your story.	☐
55	Create a series of videos in your story with a CTA to check the link in your bio.	☐
56	Upload a video about the content to IGTV.	☐

REDDIT DISTRIBUTION

57	Submit a link to a relevant Subreddit.	☐
58	Create a long-form text piece of content that includes a link to the original.	☐
59	Comment on a discussion happening on a relevant post and link back to your content.	☐

60	Turn a quote from the asset into an image and upload to a Subreddit. Include the URL in the visual.	☐
61	DM people who have asked questions or shared similar content on Reddit.	☐
62	Run advertisements within Reddit driving to your asset.	☐

YOUTUBE DISTRIBUTION

63	Create a video about the same topic and link to your article in the description.	☐
64	Reference the article in a completely different video but drive people to it via the link in the description.	☐
65	Announce the new article using a short thirty- to sixty-second video about the topic.	☐
66	Share the announcement video through your LinkedIn feed.	☐
67	Create a playlist about a specific topic and include this video in it.	☐
68	Run YouTube advertisements with the video about the topic.	☐
69	Comment on other people's YouTube videos.	☐
70	Ask for "Likes" at the end of your video.	☐
71	Ask for shares at the end of your video.	☐

QUORA DISTRIBUTION

72	Research and answer questions related to your topic. Link to your asset.	☐
73	Find top answers related to similar topics and reply with value (and your asset).	☐

74 Share the direct link to your content via Quora newsfeed. ☐

75 Run ads against questions that your content answers. ☐

76 Comment on other people's Quora answers. ☐

77 Add links to your top content in your Quora profile. ☐

ONSITE DISTRIBUTION

78 Use social media share bars that allow the reader to share to the network of their choice. ☐

79 Create a handful of tweetable quotes within the text and allow people to tweet with the click of a button using ClickToTweet. ☐

80 Create a place for "Popular Posts" and link to this piece of content so organic traffic can find it while on your website. ☐

81 Create a section on your About page that links to your most popular or favorite pieces of content. ☐

COMMUNITY DISTRIBUTION

82 Submit content to these communities if you're crafting content about marketing. ☐

83 Answer questions on these communities and link back to your own articles where appropriate. ☐

84 If the forum allows, use your signature to promote your content. ☐

85 Sponsor content within the community to ensure it rises to the top. ☐

86 Host an Ask Me Anything initiative on the community. ☐

EMAIL DISTRIBUTION

87 Send out a link to your mailing list telling them that this is your latest piece of content. ☐

88 Reach out to someone with a large mailing list and ask if they'd be interested in sharing your article with their audience. ☐

89 Sponsor an industry newsletter to have your content featured within it. ☐

90 Build a newsletter and include your own content within the newsletter that you're using to share links about a specific topic. ☐

91 Update your signature for the week to include a reference to your latest article saying: "Check out my latest: [Content name here]" ☐

92 Reach out to influencers who you mention in your blog post and let them know that you've referenced their work. ☐

93 Resend your email to the people who didn't "open" the email two days later. ☐

PINTEREST DISTRIBUTION

94 Create a board all about the content you've published and pin the content there. ☐

95 Request access to post to highly active and engaged Pinterest boards and pin your content to the ones that are relevant. ☐

96 Search for the names of people who have a large following on Pinterest and reach out to them with a link. ☐

MISCELLANEOUS DISTRIBUTION

97 Upload your content to Scoop.it and share it to communities that are relevant to your audience. ☐

98 Leverage Start A Fire as a way to drive users to your content even though you're curating and distributing content from other sources. ☐

99 Use Triberr—it's a community of bloggers and writers who read and share content with individuals with similar interests. ☐

100 Use HARO to find a story that is relevant to a piece of content you've developed. Write a thoughtful response and include a link. ☐

101 Submit to Quuu, The Juice, Zest, or another aggregator for distribution. ☐

102 Go on relevant podcasts and promote your content as a part of the interview. ☐

103 Take part in online summits and promote your content at the end of your interview or presentation. ☐

104 Join industry-related Slack channels and share within those groups. ☐

105 Share via your internal communication tool (Slack, Email, Yammer, etc.). ☐

106 Ask sales to share with existing prospects. ☐

107 Use in-app notifications to let people know about your new content. ☐

108 Use a live-chat plugin to announce the article to customers/users. ☐

109 Reference your own asset during conferences and presentations.	☐
110 Include references to the content via brochures and materials.	☑

If it would be helpful to have this list as a spreadsheet file, you can visit *thedistributionchecklist.com*.

Not everyone needs to clean their home in the same way, just as you won't distribute your content the same way as everyone else. Hopefully, you can customize a to-do list based on this checklist. With over 100-plus ways to distribute your content online, my hope is that you can tailor and implement your own plan of attack.

Now that you have a checklist, it's time to do something with it. How you might proceed in using the checklist is rooted in three preliminary distribution steps.

PLAY 2: DISTRIBUTION FIRST STEPS

If you are looking to supplement your checklist with a more conceptual place to start, all good distribution plans are formed from three foundational and broad first steps: (1) understanding what's possible, (2) researching your audience, and (3) developing a strategy that works for you.

Step 1: Understanding What's Possible

Most marketers have no idea where to start when it comes to content distribution. It's a foreign concept. In many cases, they've grown so familiar with the mindset of valuing output over everything else that they hardly spend any time promoting the content they create. It's a major mistake.

Stop thinking the lifecycle of a piece of content ends when you press publish. You won't go far tweeting once on Twitter and calling it a day. Agencies and freelancers over-prioritize content and under-prioritize the post-creation distribution processes. Content needs a pipeline from creation to consumer. That's what marketing does, and marketing is distribution. Ensure the content you create is aligned with your intent to scale your reach and revenue by distributing.

As I've said earlier, embrace the opportunity of distribution by, first and foremost, understanding it has never been more prominently available to anybody with an internet connection. If you're still not sold on the power of distribution, go back to Chapter 1 and read its pages again.

Step 2: Research Your Audience

Once you have gotten over the mental roadblocks and realize that yes, you are capable of scalable distribution of your content, now you need to get to know your target audience.

Not every audience is the same, and it's on you to determine who yours is. Strategies involved have been peppered throughout this book, but you can lead with some foundational questions.

- What analytics tools can you use to find out more about your audience?
- What can you learn organically by using the Sherlock Homeboy Method?
- What channels do they spend their time on?
- What types of content work well on those channels?
- What types of content do they prefer in general?
- What are their pain points?
- How does your content offer them a solution?
- What types of searches are they inputting into search engines?

These questions can be reasked, to some degree, when honing in on specific distribution channels. Take Reddit. Millions of users are on Reddit and find their communities in various subreddits. There are CEOs, accountants, window washers, and sixteen-year-olds trying to get better at Fortnite all using Reddit. It's a dynamic and diverse place. Which is your audience and which subreddits are they in? Take the time to find out this information and discover where they gather. Then do this on the other channels. You don't have to be everywhere, but you need to know all the places your audience hangs out.

The more you know about your audience, the better you can tailor your Content Distribution Checklist to your needs. This will help you refine your distribution strategy, how you create new content, and how you remix and republish old content.

The more streamlined your checklist becomes, the better the chance your traffic and revenue will begin to grow.

Step 3: Develop a Personalized Strategy

You know what is possible, where your audience is, and how that information will whittle down your checklist. Now it's time to build out a prioritized plan.

At first, you should make it your aim to simply complete the items on your personalized checklist. As you accomplish these tasks, start collecting data about the results. Then, use that information to revise and refine your strategy until you find the right order and combination of distribution tasks that optimize engagement with your content.

When collecting and analyzing your data, use some of these potentially applicable questions to drive your problem-solving efforts:

- What channels are most worth distributing content on?
- What types of content are worth distributing on these channels?
- What metrics should be prioritized to achieve success?
- What content should be prioritized to maximize success?
- What channels should be prioritized to maximize success?
- What are the resourcing and workflows needed to unlock success?

At first, your distribution strategy might not be able to fully answer these questions. As the data rolls in, a successful strategy will mean all of these questions are easily answered. As you come up with better and better answers, your strategy will become more and more refined, priming it for success.

Notice, also, that these questions use the word "channels," plural. Based on that research and tailored checklist, be intentional about personalizing a varied strategy that does not lean too heavily into one distribution channel.

When all three steps are realized, it sets you up for a longer, self-directing journey of growth. Once that journey gets going, you'll be better off for it. Set your own direction and let your creativity shine.

PLAY 3: THE CALENDAR

Setting up a calendar for one piece of content can be a cheat code for distribution. It guides you on what to do and when to do it.

I've already discussed the importance of coming up with a prioritized and optimized order of tasks for your distribution strategy. Putting that prioritized order into a manageable weekly schedule brings you one step closer to executing your plan.

Schedules provide a clear path forward. They are tactical. They put the playbook into action and help your content grow well beyond you pushing publish for the first time on a piece of content.

If you are not the person who will be executing the schedule of distribution tasks, instead handing them off to your team or somebody else within your organization, then I would encourage you to pass this schedule off to them. If you *are* the person who will be executing your plan, fold the top corner of this page. Keep this page or save this example calendar for your future use.

Before we get to the actual calendar, some execution guidance: You would do well to actually incorporate this into your working calendar, whether that's Google Calendar or a moleskin you keep in your top drawer. For each day on the calendar, block off fifteen to thirty minutes to ensure you follow the steps to amplify your content. For distributing one piece of content, here is a straightforward weekly calendar.

Day One: Amplification on Social
- Share on Twitter with a headline
- Share on Twitter as a thread
- Share on LinkedIn with long-form post
- Share on Facebook Page with three to four sentences

Day Two: Amplify through Native Channels
- Upload and publish as a *Medium* article
- Upload and publish as a LinkedIn article
- Retweet the original thread from yesterday

Day Three: Community Driven Distribution
- Amplify in a Slack channel
- Amplify in a Facebook Group
- Amplify in a Discord Server
- Submit to two industry forums

Day Four: Newsletters and Mixing Things Up
- Reshare link on Twitter
- Share link of your Instagram story
- Reach out to friendlies for engagement

- Promote internally for employee advocacy
- Write scripts for leads
- Add to your email signature for the week

Day Five: Influencers Outreach Efforts
- Reach out to Industry Newsletters
- DM Industry influencers with a link included
- Pin post to article at the top of your channels
- Respond to influencers' Tweets with your linked asset (adding value)
- Engage a TikToker to create content about the asset

Day Six: Remixing and Republishing Time
- Turn the blog post into a YouTube video
- Turn the blog post into an Instagram carousel
- Turn the blog post into a LinkedIn document
- Turn the blog post into a Slideshare Deck
- Turn the blog post into a vertical video

Like the checklist, this example schedule is not necessarily universal. The specifics can be tailored based on your final distribution checklist (such as what channels you will and will not be distributing on).

In time, you'll find this process becomes cyclical. Your content will start building off itself and give your target audience consistent and frequent value across multiple channels. Truly, you'll be arming yourself with the ability to create once and distribute forever.

PLAY 4: MAKING TIME FOR DISTRIBUTION

When I talk with people about the difficulties of distribution, I'm often surprised by what is identified as the biggest obstacle: not having enough time. Like many other obstacles, though, the idea of not having enough time is an illusory problem.

As part of your distribution playbook, let's go over some basic ways in which you can reduce the total amount of time you spend on a distribution strategy. This is a non-exhaustive list of ways in which you can make time for distribution.

Schedule Content in Advance

Right now, as I've been spending my day writing this chapter, I've simultaneously sent out a handful of tweets, posted multiple times on LinkedIn, and shared a few photos on Instagram.

How is it possible that my content is distributing itself while I work on other things? Through my favorite distribution shortcut: scheduling my content in advance. I have content scheduled for weeks, months, and years into the future. As mentioned, I currently have a tweet scheduled for 2083 for my kids. (Remember, please don't tell them.)

A scheduling strategy can be leveraged through a handful of different scheduling tools. My scheduler of choice is Buffer, but there are hundreds of other options. As a savvy internet user, I encourage you to do some of your own research, try some demos, and pick the app that you believe will work best for your preference.

Proactive Distribution vs. Reaction Distribution

For some channels, such as Facebook Groups or Reddit, distribution is naturally reactive. In these kinds of spaces, the rules or expectations are for you to seed content only if the community's topic gives you the natural opportunity to share a link. That's fine, and you should always look for these reactive opportunities.

Overall and in general, however, you should be looking to adopt a proactive, looking-into-the-future approach with your distribution strategy. Clarify for yourself or your team what piece of content will be shared, through what channels, and when. Which old content are you repurposing this week? Be proactive about scheduling time to go into specific channels or communities to search for reactive distribution opportunities.

Make plans. Execute plans.

Creating a Team of Distributors

As I've mentioned throughout the book, if you want to go fast, go alone, but if you want to go far, go together. When it comes to content marketing and distribution, especially as your content grows its reach, it can be very difficult to do everything by yourself. That means, at the appropriate time, you should consider making time to distribute your content through your team.

In the future, I believe there will be entire departments dedicated to distribution. The day will come when there will be a CDO, or Chief Distribution Office, at most organizations. They and their team will be measured by their ability to get the organization's assets spread on channels like Reddit, Quora, and the like.

When it comes to building your team, identify people who may have skills in storytelling for the digital age, as a social media manager, and in copywriting. Their functions as your employees are entirely up to you, but from my experience, these roles tend to evolve nicely into a distribution-expert path. Maybe they help you repurpose or remix content, such as the video editing required to transform a blog post into a YouTube video. Or, maybe you completely hand off distribution duties and let them run the entire engine.

Reducing Content Output

A lot of creators spend countless hours creating, creating, creating. I suppose creating content is implied in the name "content marketing." As we now know, however, content is not king. Distribution is. Although you may still carry around a business card that says Content Marketer or something like that, it could just as easily read Distributor.

As the market relies more on distribution, think about scaling back the amount of time you spend creating new content. To start out, my advice is that brands should split their time equally between content creation and content distribution. As your content takes off with your audience, you can scale that back even further. It means you have created the blockbuster films and can start living off the proceeds of the subsequent sequels.

When your content starts taking hold, and you start doing extremely well, I would suggest spending 20 percent of your time creating new content and 80 percent distributing. You can spend one or two hours creating a piece of content, but if that content has value, it should continue to generate revenue forever. And the more you focus on distributing that content, the higher your return on investment.

A WELL-OILED MACHINE

If you create a schedule, refine a checklist, follow the first three steps of strong distribution, and find the time to distribute consistently, you will have implemented a one-way road to successful distribution.

Not only that, but you will have set yourself up for consistent implementation and improvement of your distribution strategy. As it continues to be refined, you can expect that someday soon your playbook will operate like a well-oiled machine.

As you leave this book behind and start your adventure, I hope you feel armed with something that you can use for years to come. And you can always come back to this playbook to reset or remind yourself how to get started again. Not every apartment cleaning is the same, after all.

CONCLUSION

Without online distribution, I might still be in my parents' basement playing Madden and honing my Fantasy
Football strategies. I wouldn't have my family, my life, my
career, or the amazing experiences I've received from distributing my work. The high school version of me—"Shy
Ross," as I was deemed by my friends—would never have
matured into an outgoing marketing professional running
a multimillion-dollar business with clients that are a blend
of household and boardroom names from all over the globe.

The importance of distribution goes beyond money,
though. Distributing your stories, in effect, is part of your

story. By creating, distributing, remixing, and redistributing your content, your story will become entirely different and entirely your own. No one is going to distribute your story for you (yet), just as nobody will live your life for you. You can open up the pathways you most desire—whether that be travel, shaping industry, or anything else—by simply embracing the power of distribution and making the investment. Don't let the opportunity slip through your fingers.

If you're reading this, chances are you are a creator or entrepreneur of some kind. You've written insightful blog posts, have an innovative idea for a product, produced a well-edited video, or succeeded in creating something you want to talk about. You might be a harsh self-critic and think your content is mediocre at best. Or you may look at your creations with rose-tinted glass. Either way, I'm here to tell you a truth you need to embrace that goes beyond your biases.

You've either created some amazing things or what you're going to create next is likely going to be ridiculously valuable to someone.

Most reading this already have valuable content sitting on a drive or USB. And the world needs it. Someone is struggling with something right now because you're not relentless enough to promote your work. To put it another way, you've created it once. Now it's time to distribute it forever.

As someone who loves the power of stories and distribution, I walk around each day with a kind of existential dread. I can't help but think to myself, "There will be many people who die this year with amazing ideas and content the world would benefit from, yet it will never be promoted or distributed properly. It will die with them, never to see the light of day."

Apologies for momentarily getting dark. But that dreadful thought has a positive flipside. Now that you have a basic education on distribution, you are going to live the rest of your life as somebody who will walk around knowing you've amplified something valuable. You will have distributed your work. You will have contributed to the world.

That contribution is what makes distribution worthwhile. Every single day, billions of people go online to find things they value. With your work available and out there, even if only the tiniest of fractions of those folks find your work, you can help thousands upon thousands. That is my hope for you. It is a rewarding feeling, and it can also make you or your company generate great returns.

Let's end this here because I want you to put this book down, print out the distribution playbook, look over the checklist, and begin to distribute your content. The world is waiting, and I'm rooting for you.

Create once, distribute forever.

You've got this.

ACKNOWLEDGMENTS

Thank you to my partner and crime—a.k.a. the Bonnie to my Clyde—my wife, Kristen. Thank you for being my partner in this wild journey called life and always pushing me to strive to be the best version of me that I can be. Thank you for being the best partner I could ever ask for and helping me walk with confidence and pride.

Thank you to my little ones for keeping me inspired to write, edit, and repurpose content for so many nights and so many years. Aaliyah, Isabelle, and Reggie: I love you all.

Thank you to my parents, who instilled in me a passion for learning and exploring new ideas. Without their guidance, I wouldn't be where I am today.

To my siblings and the many family members who encouraged and entertained my ideas of entrepreneurship from a very young age, I thank you. Thanks for the love. Thanks for the support. Thanks for showing up. Thanks for celebrating. Thanks for sharing. Thanks for liking. And thanks for all you did to make me push boundaries.

Lastly, thank you to all the others who have been part of this journey—from the friends that provided support, to the mentors that provided advice. And to all the teachers that told me I'd never amount to nothing, I love you all.

ABOUT THE AUTHOR

Ross Simmonds is an entrepreneur and marketing strategist who helps brands utilize content marketing, social media, and digital channels to achieve their business goals. He's the founder of Foundation Marketing, a B2B content marketing agency that combines data and creativity to support successful and ambitious software brands. Named one of the most influential marketers in the world by multiple marketing publications and firms, Ross has received the Harry Jerome Young Entrepreneur Award and has been named one of the Top 50 CEOs in Atlantic Canada. He's been published or featured in *Forbes*, *HuffPost*, and

VentureBeat, and on BET and CBC, among other media outlets. He enjoys traveling and is a frequent speaker at global digital marketing conferences for small, medium, and enterprise brands.

Made in the USA
Middletown, DE
19 June 2024

56035293R00191